EXPLORATIONS 8

Theological and Pastoral Responses to Homosexuality

EXPLORATIONS 8

Theological and Pastoral Responses to Homosexuality

B G Webb
General Editor

Published edition copyright © Openbook Publishers 1994
Text copyright © Moore Theological College 1994

All rights reserved. No part of this publication may be reproduced in any form or by any means without prior permission in writing from the publisher.

First printing May 1994
02 01 00 99 98 97 96 95 94   9 8 7 6 5 4 3 2 1

National Library of Australia
Cataloguing-in-Publication entry

Theological and pastoral responses to homosexuality.

ISBN 0 85910 699 3.

1. Homosexuality — Religious aspects — Christianity. 2. Homosexuality — Religious aspects — Christianity — History. 3. Homosexuality — Moral and ethical aspects. I Webb, B.G. II. Moore Theological College. (Series: Explorations (Sydney, N.S.W.); 8).

261.835766

Typeset by Moore Theological College in 10pt Bookman
Printed and published by
Openbook Publishers
205 Halifax Street
Adelaide, South Australia   0574-94

CONTENTS

Preface	vii
Abbreviations	ix
Andrew Shead	
Homosexuality and the church: historical survey	1
Barry Webb	
Homosexuality in Scripture	65
Philip Mitchell	
Medical and psychological perspectives	105
Michael Hill	
Homosexuality and ethics	123
Bill Andersen	
The re-orientation of homosexuals and models of therapy	145
Michael Corbett-Jones	
The theory and practice of the Anglican Counselling Centre	163
David Peterson	
Counselling the church	179

PREFACE

There can be no doubt of the importance of the issue of homosexuality both inside and outside the church. Many Christians are actively supporting the call for practising homosexuals to be recognised as having an authentically Christian lifestyle and even to be ordained to the ministry. An extensive literature of interpretation and discussion has come into existence to support this call.

We ought always to be ready to review our understanding of Scripture, including both its interpretation and its application. In 1993, therefore, at its annual School of Theology, the Moore College Faculty undertook a serious study of the subject. The foundation of the discussion was a literature review by Andrew Shead and a biblical paper from Barry Webb. Other papers from medical, psychological, ethical and pastoral perspectives were contributed by members of the faculty and other scholars.

The papers presented at the School are the substance of this edition of *Explorations*. We publish this with the prayer that they will be of great value to the Christian community as we seek to shape our response to debate in the light of God's Word.

Peter Jensen
Principal
Moore Theological College
November, 1993.

ABBREVIATIONS USED IN THIS BOOK

IVP	Inter-Varsity Press
JETS	Journal of the Evangelical Theological Society
NICNT	New International Commentary on the New Testament
NICOT	New International Commentary on the Old Testament
NT	New Testament
OT	Old Testament
RSV	Revised Stanard Version
SCM	Student Christian Movement

HOMOSEXUALITY AND THE CHURCH: HISTORY OF THE DEBATE

Andrew Shead
Lecturer in Biblical Studies, Moore College

Synopsis

In the second half of this century social perceptions of homosexuality have begun to change, and since the start of the gay liberation movement in 1969 these changes have accelerated to the point where, in the 1990's, gay issues are a significant force shaping the basic values and structures of our society, from the family right through to political institutions. This paper seeks to trace these changes and then to assess the debate within the church as it fits within the broader framework of social change. It will be seen that changing attitudes within the church, and most of all within the ranks of its theologians and leaders, have either moved in step with society in general or have altered in explicit reaction to social change. The paper will then turn to the debate in more detail, seeking to survey the range of views held in the areas of exegesis, theology, hermeneutics and ethics. The attitudes generated by these views range from punitive rejection of homosexuality through to unqualified acceptance. Some assessment of the debate will be made throughout the paper, but we shall be more concerned to isolate the issues arising from it which warrant fuller investigation elsewhere. In the light of the fact that this is a resource paper, a substantial bibliography has been appended.

I. INTRODUCTION

Terminology and politics

The terms of the homosexuality debate have become very confused over the years. Various interest groups have used words in restricted or special senses, often from ideological or political considerations. However, the same terms have also been used to make sweeping generalisations, and for equally ideological reasons. The result is that contradictory conclusions can be drawn from identical statements, because of the ambiguity of the terminology. Therefore, for the purposes of this paper, the key terms of the debate will be defined and used as follows.

Homosexuality This term has been used in various ways over the years, but in theological circles it has come to be used in a broad sense to indicate a sexual orientation toward those of the same sex, whether or not this orientation is expressed in sexual acts. But what precisely does it mean to be 'homosexual'? Is it an either/or classification over against 'heterosexual' or is there a spectrum in society (as Moberly, 1983 proposes) from the exclusively homosexual at one end, through the mainly homosexual, the bisexual and the mainly heterosexual to the exclusively heterosexual at the other end? If this is so, where on the spectrum does most of the 'heterosexual' population fit?

The concept of a spectrum derives from the scale developed by Kinsey in 1948 for use in his study of male sexual behaviour. The Kinsey scale 'appeared to present something like a normal distribution, with the implication that most people are actually centrally placed and bisexual' (Court 1992, 10). But his scale was 'developed before any data had actually been generated and these have then been fitted to the scale which Kinsey conceived' (ibid., 6). Later studies, even those seeking to establish a genetic basis for homosexuality, suggest the existence of just two categories—heterosexual and homosexual—as a more likely pattern of occurrence than the continuous spectrum of Kinsey (ibid., 11). However, Coleman (1984) observes that homosexuality is diverse; there are different levels, for example, of sexual interest and of feelings about one's own homosexuality.

A full discussion of the frequency of homosexuality is beyond the scope of this paper.

> Suffice it to say that Kinsey's three figures of 4% exclusively homosexual, 10% predominantly so and 37% with a post-pubertal homosexual experience to orgasm have been discredited by subsequent studies: eg, a 1970 study of 1458 American men aged over 21; a 1989 study of 480 British males from 15 to 49; a 1992 study of 34706 Minnesota high school students (Remafedi et. al., 1992); a 1991 study of 2000 Hawaiians; a 1989 Dutch national random sample of male and female sexual behaviour; a 1992 French survey of over 20000 people; and a 1992 British survey of 18876 men and women (Johnson et. al., 1992). These studies suggest figures for men closer to 1% having had homosexual intercourse in the last 12 months, and 4-8% having had any homosexual experience in adulthood. For the school students the figures were 0.2% and 1% respectively. And in the survey with the largest percentage results, less than 1 in 200 women considered themselves lesbian. Furthermore, 'Many of them say their choice of lesbianism was as much a feminist statement as a sexual one' (*Newsweek*, 24/2/92, p. 48). (Court, 1992, Gudel, 1992)

Two observations are worth making: first, the 10% figure which is so often quoted has a strongly political orientation behind it. It is used to impress politicians with the size of the vote at stake, and to convince society of the normality of homosexuality. Second, the claim that 'up to half of the population of homosexual persons is female' (Spong, 1988, 197) is wildly inaccurate. The actual figures suggest that lesbianism springs from different causes and concerns, and may well need to be addressed in a separate paper, dealing with sexual abuse and feminism rather than sexual orientation.

Gay, Lesbian These words are political words and are used differently from 'homosexual', though they overlap with it in meaning.

> [I]t is a distinction that those in the gay and lesbian movement would themselves acknowledge... The task force on the Status of Lesbian and Gay Psychologists which operates through the American Psychological Association [APA] says that gay must be defined in terms of a value system, "the emerging definition of gay and lesbian is different from that of homosexual....Gay is proud, angry, open, visible, political, healthy, and all the positive things that homosexual is not" (Rekers, 1982, pp 50-51). More recently,

that Task Force has been pressing for the abandonment of the word homosexual by psychologists in favour of gay and lesbian (*American Psychologist*, 1991, 46/9, 973). The gay activist group is the most visible, the most powerful in our society, in seeking to change attitudes toward sexuality. It does not follow that it represents all those who call themselves homosexual... (Court, 1992, 3f).

In the revised (1993) version of the APA's diagnostic manual the word 'homosexual' has been removed altogether.

Inversion A term used first in the 1890's to describe one whose sexual instincts are inverted; an exclusive and involuntary sexual orientation toward others of the same sex.

Perversion The sexual attraction or involvement with members of the same sex of a person who is naturally heterosexual in orientation.

Orientation The direction of an individual's sexual instincts, whether toward others of the same sex or the opposite sex, as opposed to the expression of those instincts.

Act The expression of an individual's sexual orientation in explicit sexual activity; genital activity is usually meant. Some distinguish between homosexual behaviour and homogenital behaviour, the former being a broader category than the latter.

Homosexuality and social change: a time-line

1869 The first gay liberation movement in modern times began, with the coining of the word 'homosexual' by Benkert, a Hungarian scholar who wrote under the name Kertbeny. The movement was mainly a European one, drawing support from Germany in particular (Horner 1981, viii). By the end of the nineteenth century sexual acts between adult males had been decriminalised in Italy, France and Spain (Dicker 1985, 60).

1930-1938 The movement was wiped out by Hitler's purges and concentration camps well before the beginning of World War II.

1948 Publication of *Sexual Behaviour in the Human Male* by Alfred Kinsey. He claimed that 37% of the U.S. male population have some homosexual orientation, though only 4% are exclusively homosexual.

1950 The Mattachine Society was formed: America's first major homophile organisation.

1952 A call for legalisation of homosexuality appeared in the Journal *Theology* (Dowell, 1952).

1954 Publication of a pioneering study by Evelyn Hooker of 30 homosexual and 30 heterosexual men which influenced the medical decision that homosexuality in and of itself is not an illness (Scanzoni and Mollenkott, 1978, 82-3).

1956 The Roman Catholic *Griffin Report* declared that homosexual behaviour between consenting adults in private is not a concern of criminal law (cited in Smith 1968, 7n).

1957 *The Wolfenden Report* issued in England. Based on a 1954 meeting of Physicians and Anglican clergy, it recommended that homosexual behaviour between consenting adults in private no longer be considered a crime. This provoked debate over the function of the law: should it be creative and foster ideals? See discussion in Atkinson 1965, 136-40. Around this time the Homosexual Law Reform Society was formed (Coleman, 1989, 133).

1967 *The Wolfenden Report*'s recommendation was adopted by Parliament in England. In Australia a nationwide survey on homosexuality indicated that the majority of respondents disapproved of the legalisation of homosexual activity between consenting adults (Bull, 1991).

1969 An incident between police and patrons in a New York bar sparked the start of the Gay Liberation movement (Batchelor, 1980, 15-16).

1972 South Australia became the first Australian jurisdiction to decriminalise some homosexual acts. Further reforms in this state took place in 1975 and 1976 (Bull, 1991).

1973 Under intense pressure from the gay lobby, the American Psychiatric Association voted to remove homosexuality from the category of mental illness (Gudel, 1992, 23f). '[T]he decision to remove homosexuality from the category of illness was based not on new scientific findings, as many have been led to believe, but on political considerations' (Nicholi, 1993, 349).

1974 In Australia a nationwide survey was carried out which showed that 54% of Australians supported homosexual law reform. 20% were against it and 20% undecided. 6% of the group did not respond. (Bull, 1991).

1977 In England, a *Sexual Offences (Amendment) Bill* calling for a lowering of the age of consent for homosexuals to 18 failed to get a second reading in the House of Lords, 'in view of the growth in activity of groups and individuals exploiting male prostitution and its attendant corruption of youth' (Green et. al. 1980, 47).

1980 In Victoria the passing of the *Crimes (Sexual Offences) Act 1980* decriminalised consensual sexual acts between persons over the age of 18 years whether male or female (Dicker, 1985, 59).

1984 In NSW, the crime of buggery was removed from section 79 of the *Crimes Act* so that consensual homosexual intercourse was legal, with the age of consent set at 18 years. (Dicker, 1985, 58).

1988 Clause 28 of the *Local Government Act* in England made the promotion of homosexuality by local authorities an offence. Leech (1988) argued that this was part of a general backlash in British society against homosexuality and the gay movement. He cited from Sunday papers covering the 1987 General Synod: 'An astonishing catalogue of homosexual corruption within the Church of England is exposed...often of the most depraved kind'. Headlines such as 'Holy Homos Escape Ban', and 'Pulpit Poofs Can Stay' were followed by comparisons between homosexuality and murder.

1989 Western Australia legalised private homosexual acts with the age of consent set at 21 years. The preamble to the legislation began by acknowledging the inappropriateness of the criminal law to intrude on people's private lives, but ended with a condemnation of homosexual acts (Bull, 1991). The Morgan Research Group conducted a repetition of the 1974 survey with 58% of Australians believing homosexual acts between consenting adults should be legal, and 34% believing they should be illegal. Only a few were undecided.

1990 Queensland State Caucus amended the Criminal Code to decriminalise consensual homosexual activity, with the age of consent set at 18 (Bull, 1991).

1991 Two studies were published in major scientific journals (Bailey et. al., 1991; Le Vay, 1991), both of which suggested that homosexuality has genetic causes.

1992 Three massive studies from France, the UK (Johnson et. al. 1992) and the USA (Remafedi, 1992) confirm the results of earlier studies (eg. Rogers, 1991) that the incidence of homosexual behaviour is closer to 1% than to the 10% figure of Kinsey.

1993 In the New South Wales Parliament the member for Bligh (an electorate with a large gay community) tabled an amendment to the *Anti-discrimination Act* aimed at the prevention of public acts of vilification of homosexuals that either threaten violence or incite others to violence. The legislation failed but was then put forward in similar form by the Attorney General. Eventually, the bill was passed.

To the date of writing, Tasmania remains the only State in which homosexual acts are a criminal offence (section 123 of the *Criminal Code Act*, 1923), but the gay lobby has filed a suit against the government in the International Court of Human Rights over the issue of discrimination.

In summary, a clear progression of change seems to be evident. Following the questioning of traditional values represented by the Kinsey report, the 1950's were a time of legal debate and of the beginning of a supportive homosexual community. The 1960's saw legal debate progress to legislation, and homosexual support progress to gay liberation. The movement was out of the closet. In the 1970's the gay movement worked to change society's social and moral perceptions of homosexuality. Its major breakthrough was the 1973 victory in the American Psychiatric Association: homosexuality was now officially a normal and thus morally neutral condition. Further, its inborn, involuntary nature meant that the social fear of the corruption of the young by homosexuals could be laid to rest, at least in theory. The 1980's saw Australia catch up with the rest of the Western world in legal reform. It is worth noting that to identify oneself as homosexual has never been an offence in any Australian state; it is homosexual acts which have been outlawed (Bull 1991). Does a 'moral majority' which is opposed to homosexuality exist in the 1990's? No one seems to know, although surveys indicate that Australia has not only become more accepting of homosexuality but is, if anything, more liberal in its attitudes than the USA.

The question of the church's role can now be raised. Where does the church fit within this framework of social change?

II. HOMOSEXUALITY AND THE CHURCHES

Events and people, 1955-1993: another time-line

Until the 1950's Protestant and Catholic churches alike tended to approach homosexuality with unqualified condemnation.[1] One representative figure of this era is Karl Barth:

1951 Barth (1961) describes homosexuality as

---

[1] One notable exception, according to Leech (1988) was a section of the Anglo-Catholic church in England, where homosexuality, though officially condemned, was tolerated in practice, even as early as the 19th century.

> the physical, psychological and social sickness, the phenomenon of perversion, decadence and decay, which can emerge when man refuses to obey the divine command...the corrupt emotional and finally physical desire in which—in a sexual union which is not and can not be genuine—man thinks that he must seek and can find in man, and woman in woman, a substitute for the despised partner...It is to be hoped that...the doctor, the pastor trained in psycho-therapy, and the legislator and the judge—for the protection of threatened youth—will put forth their best efforts. But the decisive word in Christian ethics must consist in a warning against entering upon the whole way of life which can only end in the tragedy of concrete homosexuality (166).

Working from a presupposition that the homosexual orientation is the result of a consciously chosen life-style, Barth makes no distinction between orientation and act, or between inversion and perversion.

Meanwhile, theological challenges to orthodox attitudes had begun to appear, beginning with Bailey (1955) and accelerating into the 1960's, in line with developments in science and social ethics.

1955 Publication of *Homosexuality and the Western Christian Tradition* by D. Sherwin Bailey. This foundational work condended, for the first time, that 'the Sodom story represents only the sin of inhospitality and has nothing to do with intended homosexual rape.' The book contributed significantly to the decriminalisation of homosexuality in Great Britain (Horner, 1981, 4).

1962 Helmut Thielicke argued in his *Ethics of Sex* (1962) that although a homosexual orientation is not God's will, it is not chosen, and thus a responsible homogenital relationship is acceptable. H. Kimball Jones developed this stance of qualified acceptance further in 1966, speaking of the homosexual as 'a sexually-handicapped person'.

1963 The Quaker Report (Heron, 1963) was published in England, stating that homosexuality is no better or worse than left-handedness, and argued that love cannot be confined to a pattern.

1967 Norman Pittenger, an Anglican process theologian, published his book *Time for Consent* which approves of any relationship so long as it is marked by love. Further support for full acceptance came from J. A. T. Robinson's works.

1968 Troy Perry, a Pentecostal minister, founded the Universal Fellowship of Metropolitan Community Churches (MCC). By 1985 more than 50 sister churches existed.

1969 In the USA the United Church of Christ (UCC) published *The Same Sex* (Weltge, 1969)—an anthology of articles from various disciplines asserting that no valid scientific evidence exists to prove that homosexuality per se is a mental disorder, and that homosexuality is as moral (that is, as positive, right and desirable) as heterosexuality. Also in this year Dignity, an organisation for gay Catholics, was formed.

1970 J. J. McNeill (1970), a Jesuit theologian, questioned the value of act-centred morality and encouraged the use of more personal criteria such as the relational aspect of human sexuality. He was the first major Catholic advocate of full acceptance.

The Lutheran Church in America (LCA) decreed that 'homosexuality is viewed biblically as a departure from the heterosexual structure of God's creation' (cited in Nugent and Gramick, 24). But see 1986.

1971 C. Curran (1971), another Catholic theologian, criticised McNeill and offered a mediating position between total condemnation and total acceptance. He argued that heterosexuality is ideal, but given the presence of sin in the world there will be times when homosexuality becomes objectively both good and moral, being the best that can be achieved at present.

The Diocese of Melbourne Social Questions Committee (MSQC, 1971) published a report on homosexuality in which recommendations were made to the Government of Victoria, including the decriminalisation of 'those homosexual acts committed in private between consenting males of 18 years or over' (11).

1972 The first openly practising homosexual to be ordained in a mainline denomination was ordained by the United Church of Christ (UCC) in America.

1973 The Ethics and Social Questions Committee (SSQC, 1973) to the Synod of the Church of England Sydney Diocese published a *Report on Homosexuality* which called on 'homosexuals to cease from practising homosexual acts', irrespective of how strong the urge to homosexuality may be (17). It called on the church to sympathise with, encourage and support the homosexual, and it called on the Government to maintain and improve legislation against homosexual practices (cf. 1989). There was an angry response to the report by the gay church group within CAMP (Campaign Against Moral Persecution) NSW (CAMP 1973), who demanded not only legalisation of homosexual acts but recognition of homosexual unions, rights of adoption and guardianship of children, homosexual sex-education teachers in schools and outlawing of all facilities designed to change the sexual orientation of homosexuals (10-14).

1975 An openly practising lesbian was ordained in the USA by Episcopal Bishop Paul Moore.

1976 Exodus International was formed, a Christian 'ex-gay' ministry to help people out of homosexuality. The American United Methodist Church (UMC) rejected a motion to allow the ordination of practising homosexuals. See 1981.

1977 The Catholic Theological Society of America, in strong opposition to the Vatican authorities, suggested in a report (Kosnik, et. al., 1977) that the prime purpose of sexual intercourse is creative growth for integration, not procreation or unity. See 1983, 1986.

1978 The United Presbyterian Church, USA (PCUSA) published a report from a 19 member task force which recommended (i) that the starting point for study be science, since the first task is identification of the phenomenon, (ii) that Scripture gives no clear, definite guidance on homosexuality, and (iii) that all biblical questions merge into one: 'What is the relation of the ancient Israelite view of orders of creation and the Christian view of the creative, sanctifying work of the Holy Spirit?' (p. D-62, cited in Nugent and Gramick, 1989, 22). The General Assembly rejected the report but drafted its own compromise motion, that (i) no openly homosexual candidate may be ordained, and (ii) no candidate may be asked questions about their sexual orientation.

1979 The Episcopal Church in the United States prepared a report for the 1979 General Convention in which it was recommended that there should be 'no barrier to ordaining those homosexual persons who are able and willing to conform their behaviour to that which the church affirms as wholesome' (Krody, 1979, 131). Although this was defined to exclude active homosexuality, a minority of bishops and several dioceses have supported a church blessing or sanction for homosexual partnerships.

In England, a Board for Social Responsibility working party chaired by the Bishop of Gloucester published *Homosexual Relationships* (BSR, 1979), known as the Gloucester Report, which recognises the possibility of permanent homosexual relationships. But see 1987.

1980 J. Boswell (1980) published his major work whose thesis is that homosexuality was not singled out as 'unnatural' until the thirteenth century, when it became associated (largely by historical accident) with heretical movements. The Bible itself does not condemn homsexuality.

The United Methodist Church (UMC) officially prohibited homosexual practice (Kantzer, 1980).

1981 In August 1981 a UMC bishop who had supported an openly gay minister was charged with disseminating wrong doctrine. However, the investigating committee thought it questionable 'what perspective on... homosexual activity emerges when the biblical witness as a whole is brought into interaction with tradition, experience and reason' (*Christianity Today* 1982, 44). See 1984.

A presbytery of the Victorian Synod of the Uniting Church in Australia, faced with the choice of ordaining a self-confessed, practising lesbian, deferred action and referred the question to the Standing Committee of the Assembly (Dicker, 1988, 11). See 1985.

The Social Issues sub-committee on homosexuality of the Synod of the Anglican Diocese of Sydney affirmed that 'homosexual practice is against the mind of God as revealed in the Scriptures' (Sydney 1981), and spoke hopefully of effective reorientation of homosexual Christians in the context of supportive Christian fellowship. However, a response to this report expressed uneasiness about the prospect of incorporating 'emotionally immature' homosexual people into local fellowships and suggested they receive their support through central church agencies instead (Sydney 1982a). We could find no evidence of the publication of either paper.

1982 The Standing Committee of the Synod of the Anglican Diocese of Sydney presented a report to the 1982 Synod in which was reported the provision of a counselling service for homosexuals, and the committee's opposition to the State Premier's bill aimed at decriminalisation of homosexual acts (Sydney 1982b).

1983 The first signs of official change in the Roman Catholic church appeared in the San Fransisco Senate of Priests, who declared (a) that homosexuality must be addressed by science and experience as well as by tradition, and (b) that homosexual orientation is not necessarily a form of truncated sexual development. They noted that many homosexuals experience their sexuality as right and good (cited in Nugent and Gramick, 1989, 27). But see 1986.

The National Council of Churches tabled a membership application from the MCC.

A motion was proposed (but not debated) in the Synod of the Anglican Diocese of Sydney 'that homosexuality is not a bar to any ministry of this church.' The Standing Committee of Synod subsequently produced a report on the motion (Sydney Synod, 1985) which made the distinction between act and orientation and condemned the former but not the latter. The report concluded that both active homosexuals and proponents of homosexual acts should be debarred from all ministry, including the ministry of participation in the sacraments.

1984 The UMC and the American Presbyterian Church (PCUSA) both rejected motions to allow the ordination of practising homosexuals. See 1988, 1991, 1992.

1985 180 ex-gays attended the 10th annual conference of Exodus International, and stated that heterosexuality is the norm, but that 'the evangelical church has failed to understand and deal with the problem of homosexuality' (Frame, 1985, 33).

An Assembly committee of the Uniting Church in Australia published a report on homosexuality (Dicker, 1985). It made no recommendation about homosexual acts but argued that the homosexual condition alone should be no bar either to church membership or to ordination. See 1987.

1986 The LCA published a study guide which concluded that 'this church can neither condemn, nor ignore, nor praise and affirm homosexuality' (Cited in Nugent and Gramick, 1989, 24).

The Vatican's Congregation for the Doctrine of the Faith issued a document reiterating the traditional position that homosexual behaviour is 'an intrinsic moral evil', and that the homosexual inclination is an 'objective disorder'. But the document did not claim to be an exhaustive treatment of the topic.

1987 The November 1987 General Synod of the Church of England debated a motion for the removal of practising homosexual clergy. The motion was rejected in favour of a compromise. In a court case the following year the Lesbian and Gay Christian Movement (LGCM) whose headquarters had been in an inner-city London church since 1976, was ordered to leave.

The Assembly Standing Committee of the Uniting Church in Australia, having reviewed the responses (Dicker, 1988) to a previous report on homosexuality (Dicker, 1985), noted the wide range of convictions held within the denomination and in effect left decisions over ordination to individual presbyteries, although it did affirm 'standards of celibacy in singleness and faithfulness in marriage' (Dicker, 1988, 43).

1988 The UMC reaffirmed its position that homosexual acts are incompatible with Christian teaching. But see 1991.

The Twelfth Lambeth Conference recognised the need for further study of the question of homosexuality and urged that it take account of biological, genetic and psychological research (Coleman, 1992, 226).

1989 A position paper on sexuality of the Anglican General Synod Doctrine Commission in Sydney (Gaden, 1989a) acknowledged difficulty in applying oft-quoted biblical texts to homosexuality, and seemed reluctant to make unqualified judgments about homosexual activity, but did allow that some consider homosexual activity to be sinful—a muted report compared with the outspoken 1973 statement by the Sydney Diocese.

1990 By a narrow margin the Episcopal Church in America condemned Bishop Spong's ordination of a practising homosexual, and a resolution to ordain practising gay and lesbian persons was defeated 78 votes to 74 (*Southern Cross*, Nov 1990 p.8).

Two Lutheran congregations in San Fransisco were suspended for five years by the Lutheran Evangelical Church for ordaining three homosexual people, all of whom had refused to commit themselves to celibacy (*Southern Cross*, Oct 1990 p.5).

The Methodist Church of New Zealand began a discussion of a Committee recommendation that homosexuality is not a bar to ordination. However, 'the Fijian, Samoan and Tongan sections of the Church have the clear view that for each of them, homosexuality is a bar to ordained ministry amongst their people' (Davidson, 1991, 37).

1991 A UMC committee to study homosexuality approved by 17 to 4 the withdrawal of the condemnation of homosexual practices, because there was insufficient evidence to support it and because there was no common mind on the issue in the church. See 1992.

A PCUSA special report on human sexuality recommended full acceptance including ordination of active homosexuals. 'Morally proper standards of sexual activity [are] mutuality, honesty, consent and fidelity'. Group sex as a possibly acceptable practice was not ruled out (Frame, 1991a). The report was rejected in the general assembly by a 98% majority, but was handled with ambivalence: the Assembly affirmed the authority of Scripture and the sanctity of (heterosexual) marriage, but refused to declare heterosexual marriage as 'the only God-ordained relationship for the expression of sexual intercourse' (Frame, 1991b, 37).

The editors of *Christianity Today* placed 'denominations address homosexuality issues' third on their list of top ten news stories of 1991, behind the Gulf war and the reforms in the USSR and Eastern Europe. This judgment was 'based on the stories' impact on the evangelical community' (*Christianity Today*, 1991).

1992 The English house of bishops declared (i) that clergy may not enter sexually active homophile relationships, (ii) that bishops should not search out and expose such clergy or interrogate ordination candidates about their sexual lives, and (iii) that ordination candidates who reveal they are homosexual in orientation but committed to a life of abstinence should not be rejected by their parishes (*Southern Cross*, Feb 1992 p.4).

The LCA delayed discussion and voting on a sexuality report until 1995, saying that 'no absolutistic [sic] judgments can be made' about sexual relationships between persons of like gender.

The editors of *Christian Century* (1992) placed homosexuality debates third on their list of top news stories of 1992, behind the conflicts in Yugoslavia and the U.S. elections. The events they listed are as follows :

• A PCUSA church in New York issues a pastoral call to an openly practising lesbian. However, after approval at two levels the pastoral call is invalidated by the denomination's highest judicial body (Aquino, 1992).

• The UMC General Conference rejects 60-40 a statement recommending the deletion of a clause condemning homosexual activity from their book of order.

• The American Baptist Church approves a statement declaring homosexuality incompatible with Christian teaching.

• The Southern Baptists amend their constitution to exclude churches that 'affirm, approve or endorse homosexual behaviour'—the denomination's first ever action taken to exclude churches because of doctrinal or moral (as opposed to financial) matters.

• The National Council of Churches decides not to allow the Metropolitan Community Church 'observer' status, so ending the possibility of a formal relationship with the MCC.

1993 The Anglican Synod of the diocese of Perth is to debate a report on sexuality which argues among other things that the Bible has a love ethic not a sex ethic (*Anglican Messenger*, Nov 1992). In March, an ordained homosexual priest resigned when it became clear that he was expected to live in celibacy. He claimed that 30 to 40% of Perth clergy are homosexual, some of them married with children.

Proposed legislation in the NSW Lower House against vilification of homosexual people provoked a lively debate in the Anglican magazine *Southern Cross* (Jul,

Aug, Sep 1993), with the tone by and large against the legislation.

The Papal encyclical *Veritatas Splendor* reaffirmed the Catholic Church's traditional stance against homosexual activity.

Conclusions

The changing attitudes seen in society after the war made their first impression in the ranks of theologians. The 1950's saw homophile exegesis (that is, exegesis which finds homosexual activity acceptable); the 1960's saw homophile ethics (from the qualified acceptance position of 'a sexual handicap' to full acceptance); and by the late 1960's there were homophile denominations and homophile para-church organisations. By the early 1970's Catholic scholarship had caught up with these changes. As gay rights advocates became more prominent new conservative movements emerged in opposition, such as Exodus International. Within mainline churches, there was generally tension between the more conservative denominational ruling bodies and the radical scholars and homosexual lobby groups within them: the former groups by and large took very firm stands against homosexual behaviour. Homophile church groups have made much of social change in their arguments for acceptance of homosexuality, using not only legal precedents and prevailing medical opinion, but also social movements such as feminism and pluralism.

Since the late 1970's the issue of homosexuality has risen to the front of debate in most denominations. The debate has been marked by conflict between consulting committees and the synods to which they report, and between individual congregations, bishops or dioceses and the denominations of which they are a part (e.g. the group of dissenting Episcopalian bishops and dioceses including Bishop Spong who have ordained and married homosexual people). This is not to say that denominations are unchanged in stance: the grounds of the debate have been shifting gradually, with science taking an increasingly controlling place in ethical decision-making. Many constitutions have been softened so that condemnations are muted, and admissions are made that there are factors relevant to the acceptance of homosexuality which have not yet been fully explored. In short, the doors have been left open for more drastic change.

There has been a resultant shift in the debate from arguing for issues such as the non-pathological nature of a homosexual orientation or the relationship between church and state legislation, to the drive for homosexual ordination, marriage, and adoptive parenting rights. Note for example the contrast between Smith (1968) whose paper on homosexuality focussed on questions of the culpability of homosexual orientation and the problem of applying Christian standards to civil legislation, and the *Anglican Theological Review* 72/2 (1990) which was devoted to a symposium on gay and lesbian marriage. Since 1990 the debate seems to have become greatly intensified in the USA, with gradual movement towards approval of active homosexuality. The Catholic and Anglican churches have made less progress in this direction, perhaps due to the setbacks their pro-gay groups suffered in 1986-7.

By contrast, the majority of laity would seem to be far more conservative than their governing bodies. For example, when responses were gathered from members of the Uniting Church in Australia to a report on homosexuality it was found that most respondents considered homosexual acts to be sinful in all circumstances, and there were also many who seemed to regard a homosexual orientation as sinful (Dicker, 1988, 31). Similarly, a survey of American churchgoers quoted by the head of a ministry to ex-gays (Dallas, 1992, 23) found that 75% disapprove of homosexuality, and 81% of those who frequently attend church believe homosexual acts are always immoral.

The Australian scene is by and large consistent with these trends, albeit some years behind the UK and USA. The one anomaly is probably the Anglican Diocese of Sydney. On the one hand it can be said that there has been some softening of stance: twenty years ago church statements were characterised by condemnation not only of homosexual behaviour but of any refusal to attempt reorientation, and by calls for thoroughgoing anti-homosexual legislation (perhaps this reflects the fact that Australian state governments have been 15 or 20 years behind Britain in decriminalising homosexual acts). But recent church statements have been more muted in their condemnation and eirenic in tone. On the other hand, however, two features stand out as distinctive in the diocese of Sydney. The first is that it has always tended to resist legal reform, unlike Melbourne, for example. The second is that its Synod committees tend to be more conservative than Synod itself. This is a complete reversal of the situation in other denominations and countries. However, little prominence has been given to the debate in the diocese in recent years. In the 1992 issues of the Diocesan magazine *Southern Cross* for instance, only one news story and no articles appeared which were related to the issue of homosexuality.

In summary, an analysis by Spong (1988, 81f.) of stages of acceptance of homosexuality by churches is thought-provoking. He outlines six steps as follows:

(1) The issue is discussed. This in itself is significant because '[o]ne does not debate such self-evident evils as murder, rape, arson and child molesting'.

(2) Homosexuals are declared God's children: 'hate the sin, love the sinner'.

(3) Homosexuals' civil rights, when threatened by society, are defended by the church.

(4) It is recognised that the homosexual orientation is not chosen and thus not sinful. Consequently we stop fearing that our children will be 'made homosexual'.

(5) It is recognised that the homosexual orientation is morally neutral, and the expectation of celibacy is removed.

(6) The church explores how one leads a responsible sexual life as a homosexual.

This table in the 'Appendix' on p. 54 summarises some of the key events and people mentioned above, and indicates the approximate timing of some general trends in the debate.

III. THE DEBATE

Exegesis

Genesis 19; Judges 19

D. Sherwin Bailey (1955) argued that there was 'not the least reason to believe' that homosexual practices are condemned in these passages. His grounds were two-fold. First, the word ידע 'to know', which occurs 943 occurrences in the OT, is used to refer to sexual intercourse only 10 times. Second, there is no indication from within the rest of the OT that Sodom's sin was sexual. This interpretation arose only in the 2nd century B.C. and was taken up in Philo, Josephus and Jude. The sin for which Sodom was judged was in fact inhospitality. This view has influenced all subsequent writers in the debate.

Since 1955 many counter-arguments have been offered. Stott (1990) offers the following four: (i) the adjectives used in the account ('wicked', 'vile', 'disgraceful') are inappropriate for the transgression of inhospitality, (ii) the offer of a woman (in both passages) has marked sexual connotations, (iii) of the 10 times ידע is used to mean sexual relations, six are in Genesis and one of those in Genesis 19:1-13 itself, and (iv) for those who accept the authority of the canonical Scriptures, the interpretations of Jude 7 and 1 Peter 2:6-10 cannot simply be dismissed. Kidner (1967, 137) suggests that a putative sin of inhospitality 'has the marks of special pleading, for it substitutes a trivial reason...for a serious one...The doubt created by Dr. Bailey has travelled more widely than the reasons he produces for it'.

Lance (1989) summarises the other OT references to Sodom as follows: 'the Old Testament itself when it refers to Sodom...thinks of it in one of two ways: (1) as a symbol of complete and total destruction, or (2) as an example of a society where rampant social lawlessness was widespread' (143). He cites K. Dover as saying that homosexual anal violation has been a classic way of reminding strangers, newcomers and trespassers of their subordinate status, and he concludes that Genesis 19 and Judges 19 are stories of rape and thus irrelevant to the debate.

Even if one accepts, as Wenham does, that the primary sin of the inhabitants of Sodom was 'an assault on weak and helpless visitors who according to justice and tradition they ought to have protected', it was their sinful homosexual intentions which added 'a special piquancy' to their crime (1991, 361). Perhaps it is right to question whether there is anything in the passage 'pertinent to a judgment about the morality of *consensual* homosexual intercourse' (Hays, 1991, 18, emphasis mine), but on the other hand, 'it must be noted that the city was destroyed not on account of the specific behaviour of its people toward Lot's guests, but because of habitual gross wickedness epitomised by their behaviour on this occasion' (Salier, 1984, 84).

Leviticus 18:22; 20:13

Many interpreters discount the relevance of these verses to the debate on the grounds that the context is one of ritual cleanness, and that the word תּוֹעֵבָה 'abomination', speaks of idolatry. Thus the prohibition is against cult prostitution rather than homosexual practises *per se* (Coleman, 1980). Interestingly, Bailey (1955) thought otherwise, stating that these were 'not ritual or other acts performed in the name of religion' (30). Wenham (1991) concludes that the Levitical texts condemn every type of male-male intercourse: not just pederasty, which the Egyptians, for example, seem to have condemned, but the active (secular) type of homosexuality between consenting adults that was quite respectable in the ancient world (362).

The Gloucester Report (BSR, 1979) argued that the primary aim of the laws was the preservation of the family unit in the face of idolatry and Canaanite religion. But Wenham argues otherwise (1991, 362): 'How can we explain this innovation? To ascribe this to Israelite reaction against the customs of their neighbours...in fact explains nothing. Israel did not reject all the religious and moral practices of Canaan. They accepted some and rejected others...Aversion to

Canaanite custom no more explains Israel's attitude to homosexuality than it does its preference for monotheism.' He goes on to show how the opening chapters of Genesis express many of the fundamental principles of OT law, and that '[i]t therefore seems most likely that Israel's repudiation of homosexual intercourse arises out of its doctrine of creation' (363).

Romans 1:26-27

Scholars in all camps agree that the context is idolatrous pagan behaviour. Some make much of this, for example the Gloucester Report, which maintains that Paul's concern is with what it means to be a heathen, rather than homosexuality in itself (BSR, 1979, 31-2). Bishop Carnley of Perth maintains that the context is possibly temple prostitution (Carnley, 1992, 12), but this has been refuted by almost all commentators (Hays, 1986, 186f.). In addition, some maintain (after Boswell, 1980): (i) that there is no clear condemnation of homosexual acts here because the phrase παρὰ φύσιν (where phusin means 'nature') means 'more than' or 'different from' what would occur in the normal order of things, not 'contrary to' nature; (ii) that it is reckless promiscuity which is condemned here, not loving, committed homosexual partnerships; and (iii) that the condemnation is of perversion only, not inversion. The reason for this is that only perverts can be spoken of as having 'exchanged' or 'abandoned' natural relationships, since inverts had no natural relations in the first place. It is maintained that for Paul, 'all persons are naturally heterosexual and that homosexual persons have consciously and perversely chosen to leave heterosexuality for homosexuality' (Lance, 1989, 148). Lance goes on to ask in the light of modern sexological study, 'How does it make sense any longer to hold with Paul that a person's sexual orientation is a result of their disbelief in God?' (149).

Once again criticism has been brought to bear on these interpretations. The main arguments advanced against (i) above are first, that every other occurrence of παρὰ φύσιν in

Hellenistic texts means 'contrary to nature' (this phrase is taken by conservative scholars to mean 'against God's will for the created order'); and second, that the meaning of παρά φύσιν 'is significantly determined by contextual considerations. The phrase does not by itself mean "immoral"...In Romans 1:26 however, it is precisely the context which insures that sexual acts "contrary to nature" are given a negative moral evaluation' (Hays, 1986, 199). Criticisms against (iii) above are as follows: First, Paul 'is not presenting biographical sketches of individual pagans; he is offering an apocalyptic "long view" which indicts fallen humanity as a whole. Certainly Paul does not think that each and every pagan Gentile has made a personal decision...to renounce the God of Israel and to worship idols instead!' (ibid, 200). Second, and more fundamentally, Hays argues 'that the whole conception of "sexual orientation" is an anachronism when applied to this text ...[T]o introduce a distinction entirely foreign to Paul's thought-world and then to insist that the distinction is fundamental to Paul's position...is, in short, a textbook case of "eisegesis"'(p.201). Cook on the other hand argues that Paul was hardly likely to be ignorant of the distinction between inversion and perversion given the moral climate of Corinth in particular (Cook, 1980, 307); whether he or Hays is followed, the point remains that Paul speaks not in categories of orientation but of act.

A more extreme version of Cook's argument is advanced by Bahnsen (1978), who argues not only that Paul was aware of the orientation-action distinction, but that he condemns both orientation and action. In Romans 1 Paul condemns 'overt homosexual practices', but then his censure 'extends specifically to the homosexual's being "inflamed with desire"' (p.68). Because he believes the homosexual orientation itself to be sinful, Bahnsen's conclusion is that 'homosexuality is a willful orientation and adopted way of life that can be changed' (p.81). The problem with this view is that the phrase 'inflamed with desire' seems to describe something more active than an involuntary orientation.

Two final interpretations of φύσις are worth including. Following on from Boswell, Williams (1993) argues that φύσις 'does not mean natural in the sense of a fixed law in physical nature of a purely factual kind. The natural is not that which is simply observed in nature, but rather it is a human moral reflection on the natural world. It includes a sense of human judgement which can be enshrined in culture and laws' (p.108).

Some theologians have interpreted these verses in the light of 1 Corinthians 11:14, another NT argument using παρὰ φύσις. 'Nature' teaches that long hair for men is dishonourable. What is 'unnatural' about both same-sex relations and gender confusion due to appearance is that both reflect an upsetting of the hierarchical ordering of creation (Corley & Torjesen, 1987, 26; Spong 1988). The conclusion drawn is that acceptance of any reversals of this hierarchical structure, such as women's ordination or interchangeable marital roles, leads logically to an acceptance of same-sex relations.

1 Corinthians 6:9-11; 1 Timothy 1:9-11

The two words under discussion here are μαλακοί, literally, 'soft-to-touch', used of persons to mean 'effeminate', with special reference to 'catamites, men and boys who allow themselves to be misused homosexually' (Bauer et. al., 1979); and ἀρσενοκοῖται, literally, 'man-in-a-bed', for which Bauer gives the range of meanings 'a male who practises homosexuality, pederast, sodomite', and refers to D. S. Bailey (1955). Coleman (1980) argues that the situation referred to 'commercial pederasty between older men and post-pubertal boys, the most common pattern of homosexual behaviour in the classical world' (277). Nevertheless, where many conclude that only child abuse is condemned here, Coleman (1980, 277f.) concludes that Paul is repudiating homosexual behaviour in general as a vice. Scroggs (1983, 106ff.) has argued persuasively that ἀρσενοκοῖται is a translation of the Hebrew mishkav zakur ('lying with a male'), derived directly from Leviticus 18:22 and 20:13 and used in Rabbinic texts to refer to homosexual intercourse. The LXX of Leviticus 20:13 reads μετὰ ἄρσενος κοίτην γυναικός 'whoever lies with a man as with a woman'.

On the other hand, Boswell (1980, 345-53) has compiled evidence to support his alternate translation: 'a male who engages in vulgar sexual intercourse', and concludes that it does not refer to homosexuality at all. He claims that 'no Christian, Jewish or pagan writer from the period of the early church uses this word when discussing homosexuality, although they knew a wide variety of vocabulary on the subject' (cited in Lance, 1989, 146). His strongest example is that of St. John Chrysostom (late 4th cent.), who wrote extensively on the issue of homosexuality but according to Boswell never uses ἀρσενοκοῖται. Indeed, Chrysostom attacks Sodom and Gomorrah for their homosexuality, quoting from the list of vices in 1 Corinthians 6 and 1 Timothy 1, but omits ἀρσενοκοῖται. And in neither of his commentaries on these two epistles does he mention the issue of homosexuality when he deals with the passages in question. Given his opposition to homosexuality it appears that for him, ἀρσενοκοῖται did not mean 'homosexual.'

However, Boswell's case is fatally flawed, as Wright (1984) demonstrates. His patristic evidence is both fragmentary, with hundreds of references ignored, and contradictory. For example, he asserts that Eusebius of Caesarea nowhere uses the word ἀρσενοκοῖται, but later remarks that Eusebius does use the word, claiming however that it was not used to mean homosexual practice (Wright, 1984, 86). Says Hays (1986, 202) of Boswell's use of Chrysostom (albeit in conjunction with Romans 1); 'One is left wondering what an ancient writer could possibly have said to avoid being coopted in the service of Boswell's hypothesis'. Furthermore, at no time was Boswell 'able to show that the church officially taught that homosexual *actions* were morally *good*' (ibid. 92).

Conclusions

There is a range of views about the biblical evidence. For some, the Bible condemns homosexual acts as particularly heinous crimes. For others (for whom Leviticus refers to homosexuality but Genesis does not) it condemns such acts as gravely as it does any sin, but there appears to be no reason for attaching a special heinousness to these acts above and beyond other types of sin (Curran in Batchelor, 1980, 92). A few deny that there is any condemnation of homosexuality at all in the Bible. Others argue that with just four groups of references to homosexuality, there is not enough evidence to condemn it. Furthermore, the prohibitions are very specific. According to Scanzoni and Mollenkott (1978, 111), the Bible

> appears to be silent on certain...aspects of homosexuality—namely, the matter of a homosexual orientation as described by modern behavioural sciences and also the matter of a committed love relationship analogous to heterosexual monogamy. Realisation of these gaps in biblical teaching constitutes the basic reason that many Christians are reconsidering the subject.

Finally, it seems to others that the texts above constitute far too narrow a focus, and that the negative prohibitions make sense only in the context of the Bible's positive teachings on sexuality (Stott, 1990). It is a fatal weakness for his argument when Bailey (1955, 1) argues that the biblical evidence 'begins with Sodom'. Thus we turn next to the broader context of the interpretive framework for the above texts.

Theology

Genesis 1-2 and the purpose of sex

Barnhouse (1977) has made the following observations:

> What is sex for? Who may engage in it, and with whom? What sexual acts are permissible and under what circumstances? I believe that it is demonstrable that the answers to the second and third of these questions have always been contingent upon the answer to the first (133).
>
> Now in the last quarter of the twentieth century we have reached a new point in human history...[F]or the first time, it is possible to avoid reproduction safely without resorting to sexual abstinence. The full impact of these changes has yet to be appreciated...[T]he new question [is]: if the primary goal and consequence of sex is no longer reproduction, what is it? The failure...to engage this issue...has seen a rapid removal of sex from the area of ethical and moral concern (134f.).

Historically, the major attitudes to sex can be seen in Aquinas and the Reformation. For Aquinas, sexuality must be procreative to be 'according to nature'; thus, for example, homosexuality, masturbation, and sex with a post-menopausal woman are all sinful (Corley & Torjesen, 1987). The reformed tradition argued that our capacity to be attracted sexually to others is God-given, but our sexuality has God-given meaning only in the context of relationships.

Therefore, while the official Roman Catholic view is that the conjugal act is 'destined primarily by nature for the begetting of children' (Smith, 1968, 6n.), the Protestant tradition upholds 'the independent meaning of the erotic and sex element within marriage as an expression of love, not merely as a means of procreation' (Brunner, 1958, 367). Thus decisions about the purpose of sex have profound implications for the homosexual debate. For example, a group of mainstream Catholic theologians (Kosnik et. al., 1977) challenged the traditional Catholic position about the purpose of sexual intercourse, suggesting that 'creative growth for integration' rather than procreation and unity is primary. This allowed them to suggest the possibility that homosexual acts are not intrinsically wrong, but are to be evaluated in terms of their relational significance.

But what of the creation narratives? First, Genesis 1:26-28 in its presentation of Man in the image of God shows us that it is not man or woman who is the image of God, but man and woman in relationship. Second, Genesis 2:24 describes a marriage which, in the context of chapter 1, is more than bodily union; it is 'a re-union in sexual encounter' (Stott, 1990, 346). The reason Stott argues for *heterosexual* marriage is his insistence that both sexes are needed to provide the 'complementary personalities through which...the rich created oneness of human being is experienced again' (346). He concludes that no alternative to the norm of marriage is provided in Scripture. Thus traditionally, heterosexual sex is seen as providing human wholeness through both the unitive and the procreative facets of the marriage relationship.

But this tradition has been challenged in the light of the homosexual debate. Spong, for example (1988, 70f), not only feels that the advent of contraception is a challenge to the primacy of the procreative aspect of sex, but claims that the whole heterosexual norm is a flawed consequence of an obsolete patriarchalism: 'human thinking has been so influenced by patriarchal values that the male-female relationship can be imagined only in terms of a power equation involving domination and subjection. Female receptivity to male penetration in the sex act has become a paradigm and a synonym for the natural'. Clearly this view presupposes that the creation accounts are themselves a product of flawed patriarchal values.

A more challenging re-interpretation is that of Gaden. His starting point is that 'most if not all of our relationships have a sexual dimension' (1989a, 4). Further, genital activity is only a limited part of our sexual expression: 'Although...human beings reach wholeness only in relationships across the sexes, this need not be expressed genitally. It is not in the case of celibates and neither will it be in the resurrection (Mark 12:25)' (1989b, 8). From this perspective, he draws two conclusions: first, that homosexual people can achieve the wholeness pictured in Genesis 1 in (sexual) relationships with the other sex which are not genital, just as celibate people can. And second, that homosexual people can achieve the loving unity pictured in Genesis 2 through a homosexual union. Gaden supports the argument that 'a committed relationship sanctifies all sexual acts that serve to strengthen the relationship' (1989b, 7), an argument that 'focuses on the persons who are acting in a relationship rather than on their acts alone' (8). Apart from the fact that Gaden discounts the biblical sanctions against homosexuality as inapplicable to inverts, he has based his argument on a consideration of orientation rather than actions, a point that will be discussed in the assessment below.

To conclude this section we will consider some theological implications of the symbol of one flesh, focussing on the work of Bridger (1993).

The symbol of one flesh in Genesis 1–2 operates on more than one level. At the human level it symbolises the differentiation-in-unity of man and woman, and at the divine level it symbolises the differentiation-in-unity of the Holy Trinity (Bridger 1993, 120). Bridger argues that if homosexuality is accepted then both the symbol and the truth it represents collapse at four levels:

(i) Man-woman differentiation

> Human sexual ontology...is a given, not a matter of human choice...[I]t is in the intimacy of personal relationships that we discover the goal of human being. By the same token, it is through our sexuality that we relate in the most intimate way possible...The modality of personal being at the creaturely level is essentially one of differentiation from and with the other (p.120).

Homosexuality cuts across this intrinsic distinction, and thus across God's purpose.

(ii) *Purposes of sexuality* The practice of contraception does not rule out the *possibility* of procreation, and a sexual union should accept this procreative mandate in principle. Smith (1968, 3) addresses the issue as follows:

> Gen 1:26-28 stands behind Gen 2:24. There is an antecedent naturalness which is defined physiologically and expressed in the basic act of procreation within which the "relational" goal is pursued. This is not to reinstate the "conceptional" [procreational] basis of sexual polarity as the Church of Rome understands it but it is to say that such a natural possibility in the Bible provides the framework within which the relational bond is fulfilled. This is everywhere assumed by the New Testament writers.

In this context Bridger highlights the tight connection between Genesis 1 and 2 (which Gaden seems to have ignored). '[T]o contend that the unitive function of one flesh can be fulfilled in a homosexual relationship is to isolate one aspect of the symbol from the rest' (p.121).

(iii) *Sexuality and the image of God* Because the image of God is an explicit link between the human and the divine, and because it is given plurally to man and woman, the differentiation thesis is 'rooted in the divine nature'. Furthermore, the way the logic of Genesis 1–2 moves from the bestowal of the image to the command to procreate suggests that 'just as the Godhead wills to create, so man and woman are commanded to procreate: to create on behalf of God. This complex symbolism rules out any straightforward acceptance of homosexual relationships on the basis of the unitive aspect alone' (p.121f.).

(iv) *The goal of completeness* The goal of human completeness must be seen as a corporate one, not simply an individual one. Barnhouse (1979, 174) comments on this: 'sexuality itself is a symbol of wholeness, of the reconciliation of opposites, of the loving at-one-ment between God and Creation'. But homosexual relationships deny half of the image of God. Hence 'some measure of physical or partial emotional *satisfaction* may be achieved, but the Christian goal of *completeness* is not' (*ibid*).

Conclusion

To return to the historical discussion, it is clear that, depending on the way Genesis 1–3 is exegeted, different questions will emerge as crucial to the homosexual debate. If the 'Natural Law' or procreative element is stressed, the crucial question will be 'what is natural?' If the relational or unitive element is stressed, the question will be 'what is loving?' And not only this, but the broad theological constructions of human sexuality must be kept in mind as the framework within which the debate proceeds. The question one must ask of a pro-homosexual ethic is, what theological framework does it imply? And is that framework more cohesive and consistent than the traditional one? As Bridger puts it, 'what would be symbolised by the replacement of traditional one flesh imagery with same sex symbolism?' (p.122).

It will have become clear that an ethic cannot be based on exegesis and theology alone. For the way in which these activities are done depends on the attitudes of the exegete and the theologian toward their source material. Different presuppositions, different points of reference, different commitments, all colour the ways in which biblical materials are handled. It is appropriate at this stage, therefore, to consider the role of hermeneutics in the debate, and the issue of authority.

Hermeneutics and authority

Hermeneutics

Many studies, even from the pro-homosexual side, conclude that, despite the paucity of biblical evidence, it does seem 'clearly to show condemnation of homosexual behaviour' (BSR, 1979, 33). The key issue for such writers is not what the Bible says but the interpretation of the Bible's moral and ethical standards: are they timeless or not? The common position is that the text is fixed but our understanding is not. Thus the lack of a biblical concept of the 'true homosexual' and the lack of support for our distinction between orientation and act suggest that a reinterpretation is needed in the light of modern sociology, psychology, history, and other such disciplines. These disciplines give rise to several types of objection to a literal interpretation of the texts.

Even the most conservative of scholars apply principles of interpretation to the study of Scripture. At the very least, an awareness of literary type and some sort of biblical theological framework control the way a text is read. Thus, for example, the Gloucester Report of 1979 sees the NT as breaking from the OT with a new primary demand of 'unconditional love in conduct' (BSR, 1979, 36). But what governs principles of selection in the application of biblical texts? Some, for example, 'would point out that the law code that includes Leviticus 18:22 and 20:13 forbidding male homosexual acts also includes Leviticus 25:35-38 forbidding the lending of money on interest. We do not now enforce that law on Christians because it is argued that 'times and situations have changed and in our economy the interest on money is right and proper as long as the interest is not excessive' (Dicker, 1985, 21). Clearly a hermeneutic of fulfilment is needed, and a biblical theological framework within which it can operate. Similarly, Barnhouse (1977, 180-81) expresses the interpretive task as follows:

> [Interpretation of] texts referring to all kinds of sexual behaviour, requires a coherent view of biblical *principles* governing sexual relations, as well as an understanding of the significance...of sexuality in general...At the same time, it must be noted that our

> understanding of the *principles* of compassion and forgiveness must lead us to change the *rules* laid out in Scripture for the punishment of sexual offences.

Before addressing some common hermeneutical issues, the methods of Boswell (1980) should be noted, for they are very useful to 'conservative evangelical' apologists for homosexuality (such as Scanzoni and Mollenkott, 1978). Boswell blurs the distinction between exegesis and hermeneutics by harmonising the differences between the text and his own views: 'through an interpretive *tour de force*, he finds "no clear condemnation" of homosexual acts in Scripture' (Hays, 1986, 200), and thus never questions the authority of the Bible.

The four-fold classification below is taken from Stott (1990, 348ff.).

'Natural!'

It can be argued that if homosexuality were shown to be 'according to nature', then it must *ipso facto* be morally good. But there is a definitional problem: the word 'natural' is ambiguous, and has been used in quite different ways. Broadly speaking, three types of definition are used: the biological, the psychological and the theological. A detailed discussion of biology and psychology is beyond the scope of this paper, but a few points can be made:

On the biological front, there are two parts to the argument for naturalness: normality and aetiology. Concerning normality, it was argued in the introduction to this paper that in statistical terms, homosexuality is perhaps ten times rarer than Kinsey's study suggested. But even if homosexual acts are seen in 'nature' (in animals and some human cultures for example), the question is still left open as to whether 'normal' equates to 'natural' in the sense under discussion. Concerning aetiology, the argument is over the rival possibilities of a genetic, a hormonal or an environmental cause of (male) homosexuality. For many the answer to this question is highly significant. Spong, for example, in arguing for hormonal effects on the foetal brain as the cause of homosexuality, says that 'we are driven to the realisation that what we have long viewed as a moral issue is in fact an ontological issue' (1988, 77).

But how significant is biology in determining the normality of homosexuality? Court (1992, 19) states,

> The arguments for acceptance come from pieces of scientific evidence that are tenuous, flawed, and often misleading. The assumption of sheer frequency, so often used to claim legitimacy, appears to be greatly exaggerated. On all these grounds I do not find it necessary to go back to the traditional Christian teaching and reject it.

On the psychological front, it is argued that homosexuality is 'a sexual variation well within the normal range of psychological functioning' (Coleman, 1989, 114). But not all would agree. Nicholi (1993, 348) comments as follows on the American Psychiatric Association's decision to remove homosexuality from the category of mental illness: 'Thus we have the puzzling and confusing situation that if you are a homosexual and you don't like being that way, then you are sick. If you are homosexual and enjoy being homosexual, then you are well. Many psychiatrists think this to be utter nonsense'. But whether or not homosexuality is categorised as psychologically normal or not, it may be *experienced* as natural by the homosexual person: Pittenger (1976, 7) says, 'To the homosexual, the desires and habits found in that state are entirely "normal" and "natural"—and we have no way whatsoever of discovering any eternal standards of normality or naturalness from which such persons depart.' Further, the Gloucester Report of 1979 argues that nature has no fixed pattern which precludes change or development (Cook, 1980, 300). Many homosexual people do not choose their orientation, and neither can they change it.

Along the same lines, Hellwig (1987, 13) uses a relational definition of 'natural' to defend homosexual acts as good: 'when [humans] shape communities which offer liberation, happiness and fulfilling relationships to all, they fulfil the purpose of creation'. Or Spong (1988, 71): 'There is nothing unnatural about any shared love...if that experience calls both partners into a fuller state of being. Can a religious tradition that has long practised circumcision and institutionalised celibacy ever dismiss any other practice on the basis of its unnaturalness?'

However, the psycho-social arguments for naturalness have also been challenged. 'From my clinical experience', writes Nicholi (1993, 349), 'no homosexual, whether he accepts or rejects his homosexuality, really feels *or* thinks he is normal...And certainly no physician who has ever treated homosexuality for any sustained period of time thinks homosexuality normal.' And concerning irreversible orientation he writes (p.350): '[Pattison's (1980)] findings, together with the research of many other clinicians and investigators, make invalid the charge "once a homosexual, always a homosexual" '.

One response to these arguments is to try to falsify them, by showing on the one hand that biological theories are unfounded (hardly a simple or permanent solution), or on the other hand that a homosexual orientation *is* changeable and need not continue to be subjectively 'natural'—one may return to one's original 'nature' of heterosexual identity. But this will always prove hopeless, since the homosexual people who do change will be labelled bisexual by the gay lobby precisely because they *have* changed. In other words, any attempt to falsify the nature argument on these terms will fail because of the open-endedness of science and the ambiguity of experience: events do not *mean* anything; values cannot be derived from bare facts.

In the end it all comes down to the question of how God's mind is discovered. For Carnley and others it is by reason—the deciding factor must be modern scientific knowledge which 'makes it impossible simply to interpret ancient texts within the limited context of understanding of their original context' (*Anglican Messenger* Oct 1992, 12). For Pittenger it is intuitive—what is subjectively natural. On the other hand, many would argue that these are very subjective approaches which lead to a relativist ethic, and that Scripture itself must be the point of departure. The terms of the homosexuality debate assume that desire determines identity. But a biblical position must use a biblical definition of 'natural'.

'Contrary to nature' in Romans 1 means 'contrary to the intention of the Creator' (Cranfield, 1975, 125), and God's norm by creation is for heterosexual sex. To go against it is therefore called a 'perversion' (for example, bestiality in Lev 18:23). This provides the principle needed to deal with the argument that homosexuality is 'natural.' It enables the reply, firstly, that the definitions of 'natural' used above are wrong: what counts is not whether homosexuality occurs in Nature, or feels 'natural', but whether it is God's will for humanity. And once correct *values* are established we can correctly interpret the *meaning* of the events and experiences which would otherwise remain ambiguous: whether if genetic, homosexuality must be considered a disorder ('bad' in the sense that all other genetic disorders are bad) and if environmental, whether homosexuality must be considered a dysfunction, and the 'sufferer' a victim of circumstance.

Two comments in conclusion. First, it is significant that when we turn to the Bible we find that when addressing this subject it speaks exclusively in terms of acts and never in terms of sexual orientation. It is the focus on orientation that makes so much of the 'nature' debate confusing and ultimately unhelpful. Second, empirical sciences and human experience are concerned with what *is*. They have no resources within themselves to put their observations within a value-system; to move from *is* to *ought*.

'Loving!'

This has been the hermeneutical control for the studies of several major denominations, such as the Quakers (Heron, 1963), Anglicans (BSR, 1979) and Methodists. 'From Pittenger on, the essence of the homosexual lobby within the church has been the stress on the fulfilling lives that homosexual couples may have and the witness to love and hope that this expresses' (Cook, 1980, 311). Pittenger (1976) provides six marks of a loving relationship which make it morally good, whether in a heterosexual or a homosexual relationship (31ff.).

The typical pro-homosexual love hermeneutic is one that comes out of personal experiences of love and rejection which are used to create theology. For example Carroll (1991) states

> [M]y image of God as unloving father is the distortion of an unloving church that claims to speak for God...[G]ay people who have a deep spiritual hunger and need for acceptance and love are not welcome in God's house unless they are in the closet, celibate, in therapy, or "ex-gay"...The greatest sin in my life, the point of my greatest alienation from God, was trying to be something I was not and could not be...God has called me out of the closet, not only to rediscover my faith, but also to discover myself as a gay person...And finally, I have reclaimed a beautiful thought from my childhood, something from Sunday school days, a biblical image, a simple statement with the ring of truth: "God is love".

Although this is a long way from biblical Christianity, one wonders to what degree the author (and many like him) was driven to this position by a pastorally insensitive church.

Several objections against this hermeneutic should be raised:

(i) Carried to its logical conclusion this hermeneutic yields a *reductio ad absurdum*. Macourt (1977, 25) for example, hopes for a society where the range of accepted life-patterns include 'monogamy—multiple partnerships; partnerships for life—partnerships for a period of mutual growth; same-sex partners—opposite sex partners—both'. Pittenger says, 'the "one night stand" for instance, cannot be called evil in itself; there is genuine goodness there, in so far as loneliness is overcome, [and] some slight sense of companionship is given' (Green et. al., 1980, 100). And Holloway replies,

> the fallacy in personalism lies in seeing only *one* dichotomy, the dichotomy between behaviour that is personal, and behaviour that "thingifies"...There is however another dichotomy, the dichotomy between selfish and selfless behaviour...Personalists tend to assume that they are the same...The morality of sexual activity is not, for the Christian, a matter of whether it "personalises", but rather whether it achieves God's intention, namely the "one-fleshment" of the husband and wife (ibid, 100f.).

(ii) It depends on the false premise that love is both necessary and sufficient. But Jesus teaches 'if you love me you will keep my commandments' (John 14:15; cf. Rom 13:8-10).

Thus homosexual partnerships are 'incompatible with true love because they are incompatible with God's law' (Stott, 1990, 351). From Cook (1980, 308-12) we have three further objections:

(iii) The **status** of the love principle is unsound: it is strange that a principle derived from Scripture is used to reject all other principles derived from these same Scriptures. Why is *this* principle the absolute one?

(iv) The **content** of the principle is also unsound: the implied alternatives seem to be tolerant, acceptant, non-judging personalism *vs* intolerant, judgmental, stern biblicism. However, both of these positions are equally judgmental: both draw lines, both have standards, both make judgments. The difference lies in the presuppositions and the locus of final authority. The biblical concept of love is not that all is permitted. 'The fact of the matter is that both traditionally and presently Christianity is exclusive' (309).

(v) the **force** of the moral claim is unsound because it rests on motive or consequences: 'will it be loving?' 'will it be fulfilling?' But surely principles ought to be right in themselves: 'Christian morality, with its emphasis on revelation, cannot escape from the deontological element of morality' (Cook, 1980, 312).

'Cultural!'

Objections to the biblical sanctions run along two lines: (i) they address obsolete situations; they condemn practices which in their context are now discontinued, and (ii) they fail to address modern changes which have moved us beyond the range of biblical exhortations.

(i) Many exegetes argue that the biblical material on homosexuality is set within contexts such as cult prostitution, idolatry and so on, and thus do not address us today (see discussion above). Coleman (1980) tries to account for the biblical attitude to homosexuality as a reflection of the attitudes of other nations. He suggests there was a common Semitic consensus opposing homosexual practice (52-57). But Wenham (1991) refutes this, demonstrating from Mesopotamian, and to a lesser extent Hittite, Egyptian and Canaanite law (cf. Lev 18:3, 24-30) that 'homosexuality in itself is...nowhere condemned as licentiousness, as immorality, as social disorder, or as transgressing any human or divine law...That there was nothing religiously amiss with homosexual love between men is seen by the fact that they prayed for divine blessing on it' (360). AngGays (1981), a group of Anglican homosexuals in Sydney, proposed the following caveats from biblical culture: OT culture was highly patriarchal, and women held an inferior position. Thus, as 'homosexual acts seemed to involve a man playing the role of a woman, the dishonour and degradation was seen to be very great' (4). Further, 'Israel's great need for population increase in order to become a nation of significance is very closely linked with her religious understanding...Thus the "seed" was regarded as sacred, and sexual activity and procreation totally linked' (5). It follows that movement toward equality of the sexes and the fact that population growth is now a threat rather than a necessity make the biblical sanctions obsolete.

(ii) Modern changes cited include psychological findings to do with 'the place of sexuality in personal growth and development', 'the significance of sexual relationships, not any more as mainly restricted to procreation, but much more in terms of the whole interpersonal relationship', and 'the whole matter of sexual orientation (heterosexual through to homosexual), in a way unrecognised in biblical times' (ibid., 5). These psychological findings are particularly significant when it comes to the issue of celibacy. Is the choice of celibacy impossible? Is it harmful? Some argue from 1 Corinthians 7:9 that it is better for a homosexual to be active sexually than 'to burn with passion'.

Once again the main objection to these arguments comes from the doctrines of nature and creation: if heterosexual monogamy is a *created* norm, then it transcends culture and time, and thus true liberation is found only in accepting it as such (Stott, 1990, 348). It is significant that despite the limited number of relevant texts there is consistent and unqualified disapproval of homoerotic activity. 'In this respect, the issue of homosexuality differs significantly from matters such as slavery or the subordination of women, concerning which the Bible contains internal tensions and counterposed witnesses' (Hays, 1991, 19).

'Forgiven!'

AngGays (1981, 6) argues that none of us is in a position to judge others, and that '[Jesus'] willingness to be identified with the outcasts of his day is in strong contrast to the attitude of many Christians toward homosexuals...To take [celibacy] for granted rather echoes the custom of which Jesus accused the Pharisees—"to lay on others heavy burdens which they themselves would not lift one finger to bear" (Matt 23:4)'. Devor (1972) suggests that as both the homosexual and the heterosexual live in the flesh both may live by faith:

> Paul is setting forth a radical annunciation of the grace of God as a gift, which pronounces all men righteous even though and precisely while they are in the flesh...If Paul then is to be taken seriously, he would appear to be not as one who singles out homosexuals for condemnation, but rather he is one who, having branded all men as condemned, has learned to celebrate the grace of God for all (56).

He concludes, 'Could not one be graciously gay?' (58). Jennings (1977) is another supporter of this view: 'no absolute or ultimate distinction can be made between homosexuality and heterosexuality...no human condition or lifestyle is intrinsically *justified* or righteous—neither heterosexuality nor homosexuality, closed nor open marriage, celibacy nor profligacy'.

These arguments betray a basic confusion over the nature of the gospel. God does accept us as we are, but this acceptance by definition involves the indwelling of the Spirit, repentance and change. Hard hearts are *not* accepted. The conclusions made about the validity of homosexual activity do not follow from the premises of universal sin and unconditional grace. On the other hand, some such as Bahnsen (1978) would argue that even the homosexual *orientation* must be repented of and renounced. A sensitive theology is called for, lest we make category mistakes which lead us into harsh and irresponsible pastoral practices.

The issue of authority

In the 1979 Gloucester Report (BSR, 1979), the Bible was described as 'witness to the ways of God with man', but claim was also laid 'under the guidance of the Holy Spirit' to 'a liberty of judgment in discerning what God is saying to us here and now'(4). It then proceeds to judge the biblical witness by the rules of modern psychology. However, Cook (1980) in a trenchant criticism of this approach, argues that it is true we are all products of our age today as much as Paul was then. But what we make of this

> depends on a shift from describing the biblical writers as context-dependent, to evaluating that context as less significant for moral decision-making than the modern context. The problem with such a stance is that it is in itself a denial of the principle of relativism....We cannot therefore make the modern context absolute over other contexts without adding a further principle to that of cultural relativity, i.e. that modern man knows best. But does he? Even if he does, the argument from cultural relativity does not establish that. If one believes in revelation and the sovereignty of God, it seems no less likely that a revelation in a particular context may have universal and timeless application, than that modern man has arrived at an ultimate absolute which, if a difference occurs, is a basis for rejection. It depends where one's authority rests. (308-9)

In his critique of Boswell's exegesis of Romans 1, Hays (1986) concluded that

> Arguments in favour of acceptance of homosexual relations find their strongest warrants in empirical investigations and in contemporary experience. Those who defend the morality of homosexual relationships within the church may do so only by conferring upon these warrants an authority greater than the direct authority of Scripture and tradition, at least with respect to this question. (211)

Nevertheless, the task of interpreting Scripture inevitably involves the use of **tradition**, **reason** (in the form of science) and **experience**. What then, is the place of these sources of moral wisdom? Hays (1991, 20-21) points out that the first of these offers no joy to the homosexual liberationist; the second is not only ambiguous, but even if it were unequivocal it is impossible to argue simply from an 'is' to an 'ought'; and the third is greatly clouded by 'our culture's present swirling confusion about gender roles'. There is a role for these authorities (see below), but an evangelical approach will not countenance their use as a basis for ethics in opposition to the authority of Scripture. There is no psychological theory or physical evidence whose implications include a revised theology or ethic. Two examples will serve: (i) The problem of the definition of a homosexual, from which so much mileage is made in case-studies (see below), is rendered immaterial by the fact that Scripture speaks exclusively in terms of act rather than orientation. In the end it is what one *does* which provides the ground for moral judgments, not what one *is*. (ii) Were homosexuality to be proved a genetic condition with no environmental aetiology involved at all, it would not alter the Bible's judgment of the morality of homosexual activity. The Bible is clear that lack of volition does not automatically mean lack of accountability.

The place of reason and experience

Clearly an evangelical approach will not countenance the use of reason or experience as a basis for ethics in opposition to the authority of Scripture. But there would seem to be two important roles for **reason** in the form of scientific disciplines such as sociology and psychology: (i) in providing information to guide the application of biblical principles to specific situations not addressed by Scripture and (ii) in controlling the pastoral approaches taken by ministry to homosexual people. Take for example the theories of Elizabeth Moberly (1983, 1985). She suggests that homosexuality is caused by defensive detachment from the parent of the same sex during early development, which leads to a state of incomplete gender identification and ambivalence toward others of the same sex.

This is due to an unmet need for love from the same-sex parent. This love-need is eroticised when the child grows to adulthood and produces a homosexual orientation. But the same-sex relationships which occur are often destructive and self-limiting. This is because the unmet love-need of the child is coupled with a defensive detatchment from the parent who caused pain by withdrawing their love. This defense continues to operate destructively in the adult homosexual's relationships. If this theory is correct then it will affect the debate on both levels mentioned above: (i) The biblical material will be approached from a different angle. Homosexual desires will be seen as the inappropriate adult expression of legitimate developmental needs, and thus not so much wrong in themselves as not completed. The comparison of homosexual partnerships and marriage will be seen to be an irrelevancy: 'homosexual acts are prohibited, not because they repudiate the man-woman relationship, but because sexual expression is not appropriate to pre-adult relationships' (Moberly, 1983, 28). However, care must be taken to avoid forming a theology whose truth depends on the validity of a psychological theory. (ii) Pastoral approaches will match the theory. Thus what is needed is not avoidance of same-sex contact but the opposite: development of close and loving—but not sexual—relationships with members of the same sex, with the aim of becoming 'a psychologically complete member of one's own sex' (ibid., 25).

Further, it is at this stage that **experience** can become a valuable teacher, in the form of case-studies (cf. Batchelor, 1980, 7-9). So for example, reports of ex-gay Christians include such developments as: gradual change to heterosexuality, with its roots in ordinary Christian discipleship; lessening homosexual desires as a result of warm acceptance and approval from other men (Jones, 1989, Pattison et. al., 1980). However, counter-experiences can always be found, and experience-driven theory and practice will always, by definition, rest on shaky ground. What of the experience of lapsed ex-gays and homosexuals who have failed to change? Some within the gay lobby energetically proclaim that gays cannot and do not change, and provide innumerable case-studies. They say (by definition) that anyone who has changed their orientation successfully could not have been a 'real' homosexual in the first place, but had elements of bi-sexuality. On the other hand (by counter-definition), desire does not determine identity: 'just as a man's erotic interest in *Playboy* does not prove him an inevitable adulterer, so a man's erotic interest in other men does not prove him inevitably homosexual' (Batchelor, 1980, 20). In short, the very ambiguity of experience will ensure the ambivalence of any definition, theology or ethic based on experience.

Another theorist on homosexuality whose account both of its aetiology and its moral consequences is similar to Moberly is Barnhouse (1977). Barnhouse makes the point that what is most repugnant to modern sex researchers about the developmental theories of homosexual aetiology is the element of *choice* that is presupposed. Quoting Stoller she says: 'Freud believed perversion is *motivated*, i.e., that a person is somehow, in his depths, in part responsible for his perversion. The deviant act, Freud felt, is the product of the great human capacity for choice and so ultimately has a moral quality' (117).

IV. SUMMARY

Nelson (1977) suggested a model that outlines the range of positions taken toward homosexuality. It consists of the following four categories:

Rejecting-punitive

This view sees both homogenital expression *and* the homosexual orientation as sinful and prohibited by God, and its proponents expel homosexuals who cannot or will not renounce their homosexuality and change their orientation by spiritual healing or psychological counsel. It is rarely held today. The main representatives are the so-called 'Chalcedon school' of whom Bahnsen (1978) is a major spokesman. He says, 'Heterosexual desire is evil as lust (outside the marriage commitment), whereas homosexual desire is evil in itself (a perversion)' (68). And again, 'homosexual desire...may begin in various ways...but in the end it is nevertheless learned behaviour which is abhorrent to the Lord' (81). He concludes, 'Inverts must be assured that they *can* redirect their sexual desires...Since the homosexual has obviously not been given the gift of sexual abstinence, his restoration by God should eventually bring...a regaining of heterosexual desires' (91). Kelsey (1983) wrote, 'this probably is still the most common view, at least implicitly, in the actual practice of most church members' (cited in Nugent and Gramick 1989, 31). Bahnsen will not allow that any homosexual desire is ever involuntary, and therefore treats it all as wilful lust. To paraphrase Luther's words, Bahnsen expects the homosexual person not only to prevent the birds making nests in their hair, but also to ensure they do not fly overhead. He therefore treats an orientation which is sinful in the sense that it is part of a fallen creation and of original sin, as one which is also sinful in the sense that the homosexual is morally culpable for its continuing presence in his or her life.

The more extreme versions of this position support their view by citing biblical sanctions which impose the death penalty for homosexuality, and see AIDS as God's punishment. The main critique of this position is that its adherents adopt and assert biblical truths selectively. 'It is simply not enough to quote the Bible to settle the question; one must argue theologically for this or that principle of selection' (ibid., 33).

Rejecting-nonpunitive

This view rejects homogenital *acts* but not homosexual *persons*. It is the view held by the majority of denominational bodies, including the Roman Catholic and most Anglican churches. The pastoral response is to urge total abstinence where cure is impossible. In addition, many would encourage one to one stable relationships with other homosexual persons without genital expression. Some would add that 'where [genital activity] occurs periodically, provided the persons involved are genuinely but gradually striving to reach the ideal of a celibate relationship, there is no need to break off the relationship' (Nugent and Gramick 1989, 34). The grounds for this position vary: Natural Law, tradition and Scripture all suggest that homosexual acts are against God's intention for nature and thus 'intrinsically evil'. But critics argue that God's desire for our wholeness and fulfilment points to 'the moral rightness of homosexual activity when placed in the responsible service of God through the establishment of a committed and enduring relationship' (Coleman, 1984, 115). However Barth (1961) argued the other way, namely, that heterosexuality is intrinsically bound up with wholeness, and that homosexuality actually falls short of full humanness:

> [T]he male is a male in the Lord only, but precisely, to the extent that he is with the female, and the female likewise...[Their freedom] can take shape only in their fellowship with each other, and their humanity can consist concretely only in the fact that they live in fellow-humanity, male with female, and female with male...The real perversion takes place...where man will not see his partner of the opposite sex and therefore the primal form of fellow-man, refusing to hear his question and to make a responsible answer, but trying to be human in himself as sovereign man or woman, rejoicing in himself in self-satisfaction and self-sufficiency... This is the place for protest, warning and conversion. The command of God shows him irrefutably—in clear contradiction to his own theories—that as a man he can only be genuinely human with woman, or as a woman with man. In proportion as he accepts this insight, homosexuality can have no place in his life, whether in its more refined or cruder forms. (165-6).

For a pro-homosexual critique of Barth, see Nelson (1977), and Batchelor (1980), 194-6.

Qualified acceptance

This view holds that a homosexual orientation including, in some cases, genital expression, can be an acceptable way of living out the Christian life, but that it is inferior in some way to heterosexuality. Homosexuality is variously described as imperfect, essentially incomplete, non-normative, and less than ideal. Curran (1971) is a classic exponent of this view. Many church statements have taken this line, particularly sub-groups within denominations, such as the Roman Catholic Bishops of England and Wales (cited in Nugent and Gramick, 1989, 38), and advisory bodies to denominational Synods and Assemblies (e.g. the Church of England, the

Episcopalian, Methodist, Presbyterian and Lutheran churches in America). The acceptance of homosexuality is here grounded in the judgment that people do not freely choose their sexual orientation and cannot change it.

Perhaps the most convincing exponents of this position are Thielicke (1962) and Kimball Jones (1966). They see the homosexual person as 'sexually handicapped.' Helmut Thielicke for example, says that homosexuality is a perversion or disorder of the fallen world; the sufferer did not choose it, but it is a particular manifestation of the original sin in which we all share. 'The homosexual must therefore be willing to be treated or healed so far as this is possible...But now experience shows that constitutional homosexuality...is largely insusceptible to treatment' (p.283). Thielicke cites the modern concept of a homosexual 'orientation' as one which, being alien to the NT, forces us to reinterpret the relevant NT ethical teachings. Homosexual people must behave ethically *on the basis of* their irreversible orientation, and this means a responsible sexual relationship which, although it cannot fulfil God's purposes for human sexuality, can at least provide the loving fulfilment which is a goal of sex in Genesis 1-3. To put it simply, given that they are sexually handicapped, homosexual people must try to do the best that they can within their limitations.

Furthermore, Jones observed that

> If the Church is to be of any help to the homosexual, then it must begin at the point where he finds himself. Thus, the question should not be whether he is *per se* in a state of sin (are not we all!), but rather how he can make the best of a given...unchangeable situation...Such an acceptance is not an idealisation of the homosexual way of life. Thus, we could not...perform marriages between homosexuals (Batchelor, 1980, 107ff.).

This is an attractive argument on many levels, but it is fatally flawed. The focus on orientation is the first mistake. It leads to the conclusion that celibacy is not an option, by the sort of reasoning that goes, 'I am homosexual. I cannot change this. I cannot help having homosexual relationships because that is who I am.' Celibacy, on the other hand, is 'a special calling and, moreover, is an act of free will' (Thielicke, 1962, 285. See 1 Cor 7:7). But the Bible's interest is in actions, not orientation: we may not be able to alter our sexual orientation, but we are free to change our actions. To use 1 Corinthians 7 to justify homosexual activity is fallacious: Paul did not intend that a passionate heterosexual fornicate if he could not find a wife.

Finally, the mere existence of a *need* for loving fulfilment through sex is not enough. For the Gloucester Report, the fact that the needs of every individual are the concern of God leads to the conclusion that 'even if complementarity, companionship and procreation are the divine pattern for sexual relationships, there remains the problem of the sexual fulfilment of those who can never achieve this ideal with members of the opposite sex' (BSR, 1979, 301). But in response Cook (1980, 304-5), using the example of a frustrated spinster who 'needs a man', comments:

> That this is her need is not in itself a reason to meet that need. In essence, the talk of fulfilment in a relationship as *the* sole criterion by which the rightness or wrongness of an action is to be judged means that there can be no morally significant distinction between homosexual and heterosexual practices. However, in response to the question of whether we have different criteria for judging homosexual relationships as opposed to heterosexual relationships, it is perfectly possible to say that the criteria are the same. Nevertheless, there is a category of heterosexual relationship, i.e. marriage, which is of a different kind and order and forms no parallel with even the highest and best form of homosexual relationship. That context of marriage is the proper one for the exercise of genital activity in a loving, fulfilling way.

Full acceptance

This view holds that homosexuality is part of the divine plan of creation in all its diversity. Homosexual expression is as natural and good as heterosexuality. Indeed, society's development toward greater humanness needs homosexuals and lesbians (McNeill, 1987). This is the view held by a small minority of denominations (e.g. the Quakers [Heron, 1963] and the United Church of Christ in America), by many ethicists (e.g. McNeill, a Catholic; Pittenger, an Anglican) and by most gay rights organisations within denominational bodies. McNeill (1970) applied the traditional Catholic moral principle that allows the toleration of the lesser of two evils when faced with a necessary choice. Thus a stable and permanent homosexual relationship is to be accepted as a lesser evil than promiscuity. The assumption he had to make, of course, was that a life of total sexual abstinence is not always a viable alternative for particular homosexual individuals. In 1988 Episcopalian Bishop Spong took this logic one step farther by questioning the standard of abstinence for any single person, whether hetero- or homosexual.

The ethical basis for this view is that wholesome sexuality is to be evaluated in terms not of procreation but of the nature and quality of the relationship. Thus sexuality is viewed solely as a way of intercommunication, and homosexual expressions are neutral in themselves, becoming moral or immoral by their relational characteristics. Pittenger (1976) states: 'In so far as [homosexual acts] contribute to the movement of the persons toward mutual fulfilment and fulfilment in mutuality, with all the accompanying characteristics of love, they are good acts. In so far as they do not contribute toward mutual fulfilment in love, they are bad acts' (Batchelor, 1980, 141). The issue of religious ceremonies for homosexual unions becomes important at this point. To the question of how homosexuality can be procreative or 'life-serving' it is answered (i) that same-sex couples can be 'generative in their relationships so that they transcend themselves in new ways' (Nugent and Gramick, 1989, 41); and (ii) that child-rearing can also fulfil this role within homosexual partnerships. Some proponents of this view would want to move on to advocate recreational sex as valid at times, and homosexual activity as appropriate for heterosexual people on occasions (Nugent and Gramick, 1989, 41-2).

V. ASSESSMENT AND CONCLUSIONS

Assessment

Quite clearly there are aspects of the debate that are not clear-cut. To quote Lance (1989, 140f.),

> The prophets never include same-sex behaviour in their list of Israel's moral and ethical problems. The issue is never raised in

the Gospels. The first point that must be made therefore, is that the current intense interest in the issue of homosexuality and the Bible is our interest; it does not reflect the biblical priorities. A second point that needs to be clear is that there is no word...that is the equivalent of the modern word homosexuality. That the phenomenon occurred in both societies is clear; in fact it occurs in all human societies, ancient or modern. But to ask what the Bible has to say about homosexuality in the modern sense is a bit like asking what the Bible has to say about modern economic theory. There are statements in the Bible about buying, selling, cheating in the marketplace, etc.; but there are no statements about economic theory per se, for that is a modern concept.

On the other hand it would seem that a great deal of confusion is caused by inappropriate definitions. Some of the areas in which clear thinking is essential are outlined below.

'Gay' versus 'homosexual'

It is important to remember the political drive behind popular definitions of homosexuality and theories about its causes. We will often have to 'de-mythologise' the interpretations of medical and social occurrences, and be aware of biased and inaccurate use of data and statistics. On the other hand, we must beware of treating all homosexual people as gay activists. Remember the group of 'disenfranchised' homosexuals with whom we can form close bonds of Christian fellowship, and who can be an effective bridge back into the gay community for gospel outreach.

'Is' versus 'ought'

Crucial to hermeneutics is the use made of the empirical facts of science and experience. We must think carefully about valid and invalid ways of appealing to these facts in our value judgments. A moral 'ought' based on an empirical 'is' will always be arbitrary and relativistic.

'Orientation' versus 'action'

Perhaps more than any other factor, the substitution of orientation for action in ethical equations has led to confusion and ambiguity. Two examples are worth mentioning. First, consider the argument that homosexuality is 'natural'. The confusion of orientation and action will lead to the conclusion that one's homosexuality is a given of one's personality (which it is) and therefore that celibacy is not an option (a false conclusion). Second, consider the argument that homosexuality is loving; that a committed relationship sanctifies all the sexual acts that serve to strengthen that relationship. This sounds good because of its focus on relationship, but one only has to substitute a word such as 'greed' or 'aggression' to see the absurdity of valuing a relationship simply because it is an expression of inner drives of the persons concerned. Finally, it seems to this writer that the exclusive reference to sexual acts in the Bible and never to orientation is a mark of divine wisdom. Ultimately, judgments made on the basis of orientation must risk becoming arbitrary and subject to both the uncertainties of changing science and the whims and prejudices of individuals. But the Biblical focus on act can only be a bonus at the pastoral level. It gives the Christian minister great freedom both to accept homosexual persons and to guide them.

The Bible: should we change our mind?

Stott (1990) suggests three questions to be asked at the biblical level: (i) Is there a normal sexual preference which God decrees as his will? (ii) Can the Bible be shown either to sanction homosexual partnerships or not to condemn them? (iii) If not homosexual partnerships, what *does* the Bible condemn? It seems that the demonstration of a *probability* that the relevant texts refer only to deviant homosexuality is not enough. For as long as normal homosexual practices could be meant, and no positive counter-statements are made anywhere in Scripture, it seems highly likely that the condemnations actually refer to homosexual practice in general. After all, are there any precedents for the condemnation of a corrupt aspect of normal behaviour where it is not made clear, either by injunction or by example, that the normal practice of this behaviour is acceptable (e.g. adultery versus sex within marriage, stealing versus borrowing, and so on)? On similar lines, Cook (1980, 309) proposes that to cast off tradition, both its inadequacy and the superiority of the alternative must be shown. It needs to be demonstrated that the traditional position is not just distasteful to the gay lobby but is inadequate in itself, *and* that the suggested alternative is better—that is, more coherent, more consistent with the facts, more workable.

'Traditional' versus 'revisionist' theology

Bridger (1993) points out that the acceptance of homosexual behaviour comes at the cost of 'a rival way of doing theology' (p.117). He argues that acceptance of homosexual acts involves acceptance of the following:

(i) *The repudiation of a natural or created moral order.* This is the logical conclusion to be drawn from the equation of *phusis* with open-ended moral reflection by human beings upon the world as they perceive it. Thus the distinction between a God-given moral order and a humanly-constructed one disappears' (p.118).

(ii) *The switch from an objective to a subjective morality.* 'If the moral order is not objectively given by God, it must be the product of the human mind' (loc. cit.).

(iii) *A shift in the centre of theology.* '...[T]he organising centre is not theology but sociology and psychology. In interpreting Scripture, the conceptual categories supplied by these disciplines become dominant; hence the reinterpretation of Romans 1 to take account of the invert/pervert distinction' (p.119).

Pastoral issues

> The gay activist group is the most visible, the most powerful in our society, in seeking to change attitudes toward sexuality. It does not follow that it represents all those who call themselves homosexual...I believe there is a substantial disenfranchised group of homosexuals who are sad and hurt, who recognise that what they experience is not normal, and who would wish to change. This is not a group that has a public voice of its own, and will only experience advocacy from others who are willing to speak on their behalf (Court, 1992, 3f.).

Faith, hope and love

Stott (1990) encourages homosexuals to remember that faith accepts God's standards, and hope believes in change in the end; and he reminds heterosexuals that love renounces homophobia and replaces it with true relationships rather than a void for celibate homosexuality.

Hope: 'Curing' the homosexual. A. Davidson (cited in SSQC, 1973, 17) says: 'I take it that Paul's advice to converted slaves in 1 Corinthians 7—to be content to remain in slavery if it seems inevitable, but if they do get a chance of freedom, to make the most of it—is based on a principle which applies here, and that while it is certainly wrong to acquiesce in homosexual practice, it may also be wrong in this sense, to acquiesce in the homosexual condition'. If homosexuality is understood to be a function of personality, a 'disease of the soul', then it will be expected that 'some ex-gays struggle and fall and struggle again, just as other Christians do when they deal with heterosexual promiscuity, or alcoholism, or greed, or anger' (Jones, 1989, 21).

Love: (Frame, 1985): To what degree is it true that 'the evangelical church has failed to understand and deal with the problem of homosexuality'? See SSQC, 1973, 19: 'From the church the homosexual should expect to find understanding and sympathy...support and encouragement...but, on the other hand, he will not expect to be received if he does not...stop his homosexual acts, and seek to achieve with God's help such sexual reorientation as may be open to him.' On the other hand, see AngGays 1981, 7:

> The church fails to offer us support in crisis situations such as the death of a partner, breakup of a relationship, problems within a relationship. It fails to support us when we are persecuted, when we suffer job discrimination, when we are bashed and attacked...We are unable to participate fully in parish life. We must appear at church as "single people" unable to bring the context of our lives, our relationships, our households, our families, into the congregational life of the Church...We aren't allowed to incorporate our sexuality into our lives like other well-adjusted human beings...We are excluded from the prayer-life of the Church.

Even making due allowance for grievances based on the assumption that homogenital relationships are acceptable, there is still food for thought in some of these observations.

APPENDIX

HISTORY OF THE DEBATE

DATE	SOCIETY	CHURCH
1955	Legal debate (1)	D. S. Bailey: exegesis CofE involved in legal debate.
1960ff	(2)	Thielicke, Jones, Pittenger: ethics
1967	Wolfenden: legal in UK	
1969	Gay Liberation Movt. (3)	Troy Perry: MCC founded
1970f		McNeill, Curran: Catholic ethics UCC ordains a homosexual
1973	APA: 'not a disease' (4) (5)	Sydney Diocese report
1975f	Australian opinion polls favourable	Lesbian ordination in ECUSA Exodus International formed
1978ff	(6)	Committees v. Synods: debate
1980		Boswell: exegesis
1980's	Australian law reforms Incidence 1% not 10%	Various Synod reports
1990's	Genetic causes claimed	Top Christian issue in USA

The numbers in parentheses along the right hand side of the central column correspond with Spong's six stages outlined on p. 20. Once again they are only estimates.

BIBLIOGRAPHY

N.B. Where shortened titles are used they are listed in bold type in parentheses after the author(s).

'AngGays', 1981, *Judge Others? A Contribution to Discussion* (Hunters Hill).

Aquino, J., 1992, 'Gay Issues Kept Alive for Presbyterians', *Christian Century*, 109/5:118-119.

Atkinson, D.J., 1979, *Homosexuals in the Christian Fellowship* (Latimer Studies 5/6; Oxford: Latimer House). With a chapter by A. W. Steinbeck.

Atkinson, R., 1965, *Sexual Morality* (London: Hutchinson).

Bauer, W., Arndt, W.F., Gingrich, F.W., Danker, F.W. (eds), 1979, *A Greek-English Lexicon of the New Testament and Other Early Christian Literature*, 2nd ed. (Chicago: Univ. of Chicago Press).

Bahnsen, G.L., 1978, *Homosexuality: A Biblical View* (Grand Rapids: Baker).

Bailey, D.S., 1955, *Homosexuality and the Western Christian Tradition* (Hamden: Shoestring Press).

Bailey, M., & Pillard, R.C., 1991, 'A Genetic Study of Male Sexual Orientation', *Archives of General Psychiatry* 48:1089-1096.

Barnhouse, R.T., 1979, *Homosexuality: A Symbolic Confusion* (New York: Seabury Press).

Barth, K., 1961, *Church Dogmatics* Vol III part 4; Tr. G. W. Bromiley, T. F. Torrance, eds; (Edinburgh: T & T Clark).

Batchelor, E., ed., 1980, *Homosexuality and Ethics* (New York: Pilgrim Press).

Boswell, J., 1980, *Christianity, Social Tolerance and Homosexuality: Gay People in Western Europe from the Beginning of the Christian Era to the Fourteenth Century* (Chicago and London: University of Chicago Press).

Bridger, F., 1993, 'Entropy, Sexuality and Politics: A Reply to Michael Williams', *Anvil* 10/2:111-123.

Brunner, E., 1958, *The Divine Imperative* (London: Lutterworth).

Board for Social Responsibility, (**BSR**), 1979, *Homosexual Relationships: A Contribution to Discussion* (London: CIO).

Bull, M., Pinto, S., & Wilson, P., 1991, *Trends and Issues No. 29: Homosexual Law Reform in Australia* (Australian Institute of Criminology).

Campaign Against Moral Persecution, (**CAMP**), 1973, *Homosexuals Report Back: A Retort to the Report on Homosexuality of the Ethics and Social Questions Committee of the Church of England Diocese of Sydney* (Sydney).

Carnley, P., 1992, Oct.,'"Beat-up" Causes Heavy Thinking', *Anglican Messenger*, 12.

Carroll, W., 1991, 'God as Unloving Father' *Christian Century* 108/8:255-256.

Christian Century, 1991, Mar 13, 'UMC on Homosexuality', 108/9:289-290.

Christian Century, 1992, Dec 23, 'Religious Wars, Culture Wars', 109/38:1179-1182.

Christianity Today 1982, Jul 16, 'Methodists Rule on Homosexuality', XXVI/12:44.

Christianity Today, 1991, Dec 16, 'Top News Stories of 1991' 35/15:54.

Coleman, G.D., 1984, 'Homosexuality and the Churches: An Overview', *Ecumenical Trends*, 13/8:113-116.

_____, 1987, Dec, 'The Vatican Statement on Homosexuality', *Theological Studies*, 48/4:727-734.

Coleman, P., 1980, *Christian Attitudes to Homosexuality* (London: SPCK).

_____, 1989, *Gay Christians: A Moral Dilemma* (London: SCM).

Coleman, R., ed., 1992, *Resolutions of the Twelve Lambeth Conferences 1867-1988* (Toronto: Anglican Book Centre).

Cook, E.D., 1980, 'Homosexuality: A Review of the Debate', *Churchman*, 94/4:297-313.

Corley K.E. and Torjesen, K., 1987, Mar-Apr, 'Sexuality, Hierarchy and Evangelicalism', *TSF Bulletin* , 10/4:23-25.

Court, J.H., 1986, *The Homosexual Debate: A Psychologist's Response.* Paper presented to S. A. Fellowship for Revival (Uniting Church in Australia).

_____, 1992, *Christian Attitudes to Human Sexuality With Special Reference to Homosexuality.* Text of a public address given in Auckland.

Cranfield, C.E.B., 1975, *The Epistle to the Romans.* Vol. I (Edinburgh: T & T Clark).

Curran, C., 1971, 'Homosexuality and Moral Theology: Methodological and Substantive Considerations', *The Thomist*, 30:447-481.

Dallas, J., 1992, Jun 22, 'Born Gay?' *Christianity Today*, 36/7:20-23.

Davidson, A.K., 1991, 'The Doctrinal and Historical Background', in *Homosexuality: A Christian Perspective: Lectures Given at St. Luke's Presbyterian Church, Auckland, March 1991* (Orewa: College Communications), 15-41.

Dicker, G.S., ed., 1985, *Homosexuality and the Church: A Report of the Assembly Committee on Homosexuality and the Church* (Melbourne: Uniting Church Press).

_____, ed., 1988, *Homosexuality and the Church: Responses* (Melbourne: Uniting Church Press).

De Young, J.B., 1991, Jun, 'The Contributions of the Septuagint to Biblical Sanctions Against Homosexuality', *Journal of the Evangelical Theological Society* 34/2:157-177.

Devor, R.C., 1972, May, 'Homosexuality and St. Paul' *Pastoral Psychology* 23/224:50-58.

Dowell, G., 1952, Jan, 'The Church and Homosexuals', *Theology* LV/379:28-29.

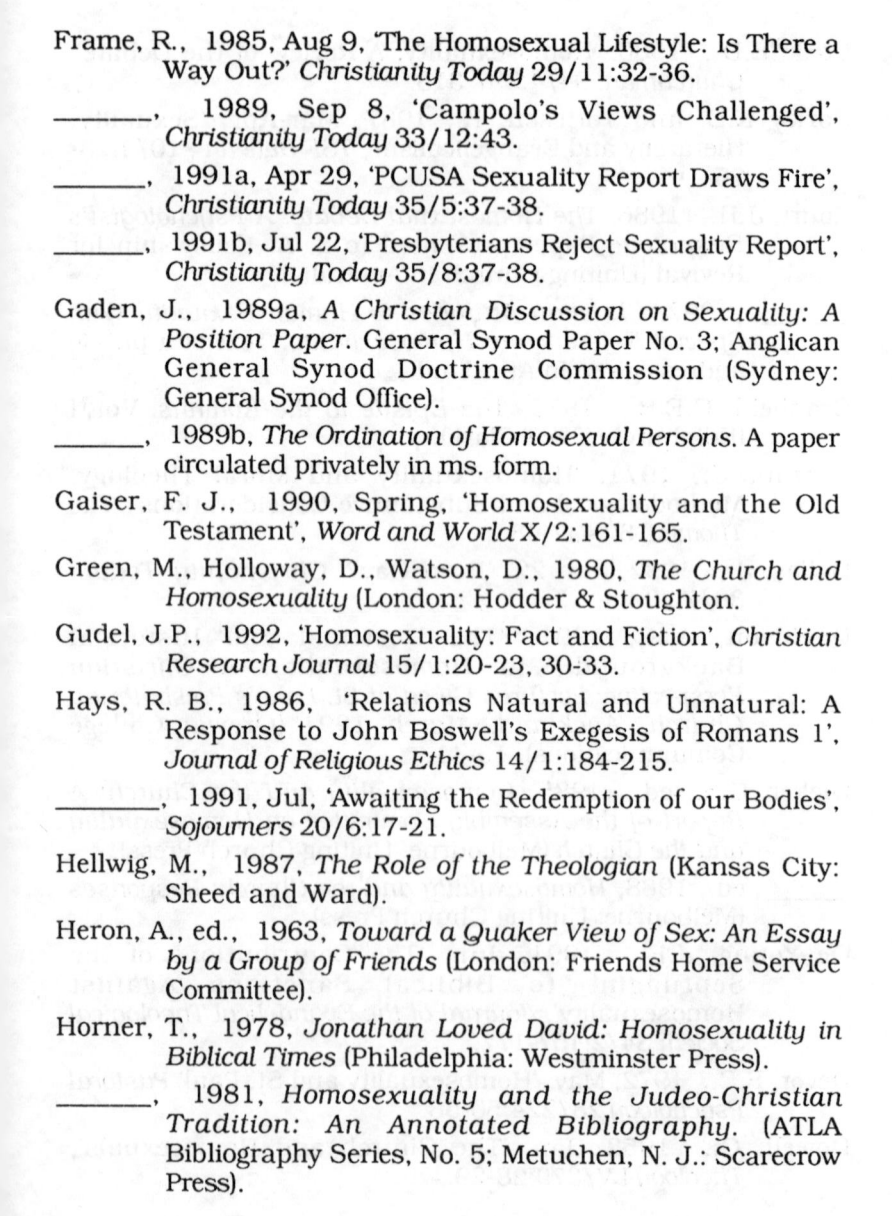

Frame, R., 1985, Aug 9, 'The Homosexual Lifestyle: Is There a Way Out?' *Christianity Today* 29/11:32-36.

———, 1989, Sep 8, 'Campolo's Views Challenged', *Christianity Today* 33/12:43.

———, 1991a, Apr 29, 'PCUSA Sexuality Report Draws Fire', *Christianity Today* 35/5:37-38.

———, 1991b, Jul 22, 'Presbyterians Reject Sexuality Report', *Christianity Today* 35/8:37-38.

Gaden, J., 1989a, *A Christian Discussion on Sexuality: A Position Paper*. General Synod Paper No. 3; Anglican General Synod Doctrine Commission (Sydney: General Synod Office).

———, 1989b, *The Ordination of Homosexual Persons*. A paper circulated privately in ms. form.

Gaiser, F. J., 1990, Spring, 'Homosexuality and the Old Testament', *Word and World* X/2:161-165.

Green, M., Holloway, D., Watson, D., 1980, *The Church and Homosexuality* (London: Hodder & Stoughton).

Gudel, J.P., 1992, 'Homosexuality: Fact and Fiction', *Christian Research Journal* 15/1:20-23, 30-33.

Hays, R. B., 1986, 'Relations Natural and Unnatural: A Response to John Boswell's Exegesis of Romans 1', *Journal of Religious Ethics* 14/1:184-215.

———, 1991, Jul, 'Awaiting the Redemption of our Bodies', *Sojourners* 20/6:17-21.

Hellwig, M., 1987, *The Role of the Theologian* (Kansas City: Sheed and Ward).

Heron, A., ed., 1963, *Toward a Quaker View of Sex: An Essay by a Group of Friends* (London: Friends Home Service Committee).

Horner, T., 1978, *Jonathan Loved David: Homosexuality in Biblical Times* (Philadelphia: Westminster Press).

———, 1981, *Homosexuality and the Judeo-Christian Tradition: An Annotated Bibliography*. (ATLA Bibliography Series, No. 5; Metuchen, N. J.: Scarecrow Press).

Johnson, A. M., Wadsworth, J., Wellings, K., Bradshaw, S., & Field, J., 1992, (Dec 3), 'Sexual Lifestyles and HIV Risk', *Nature*.

Jones, H. K., 1966, *Toward a Christian Understanding of the Homosexual* (New York: Association Press).

Jones, S. L., 1989, Aug 18, 'Homosexuality According to Science', *Christianity Today* 33/11:26-29.

Kantzer, K. S., 1980, Apr 18, 'Homosexuality: Biblical Guide Through A Moral Morass', *Christianity Today* XXIV/8:12.

Kelsey, D., 1983, 'Homosexuality and the Church: Theological Issues', *Reflection* 80/3:9-12.

Kidner, D., 1967, *Genesis* (TOTC; Leicester: IVP).

Kosnik, A., Carroll, W., Cunningham, A., Modras, R., & Schulte, J., 1977, *Human Sexuality: New Directions in American Catholic Thought* (New York: Paulist Press).

Krody, N. E., 1979, Oct, 'Human Sexuality and the Christian Churches', *Ecumenical Trends* 8/9:129-135.

Anglican Consultative Council, (**Lambeth**), 1988, *The Truth Shall Make You Free: The Lambeth Conference 1988: The Reports, Resolutions and Pastoral letters From The Bishops* (London: Church House Publishing).

Lance, H. D., 1989, 'The Bible and Homosexuality', *American Baptist Quarterly* 8/2:140-151.

LeVay, S., 1991, 'A Difference in Hypothalamic Structure between Heterosexual and Homosexual Men', *Science* 253:1034-1037.

Leech, K., 1988, Jul 20, 'Crisis For Gays in the Church of England', *Christian Century* 105/22:678-679.

Lovelace, R., 1979, *Homosexuality and the Church* (London: Lamp).

Mackey, L., 1988, Oct 7, 'Canadians Barely United on Homosexual Issue', *Christianity Today* 32/14:50.

McNeill, J. J., 1977, *The Church and the Homosexual* (London: Darton, Longman and Todd).

———, 1977, Mar 11, 'Homosexuality: Challenging the Church to Grow', *Christian Century*:242-246.

Macourt, M., ed., 1977, *Toward a Theology of Gay Liberation* (London: SCM).

Moberly, E. R., 1980, May, 'Homosexuality: Structure and Evaluation', *Theology* 53:177-184.

———, 1983, *Homosexuality: A New Christian Ethic* (Cambridge: J. Clark).

———, 1985, Jun, 'First Aid in Pastoral Care: XV. Counselling the Homosexual', *Expository Times* 96/9:261-266.

Melbourne Social Questions Committee, Diocese of, (**MSQC**), 1971, *Report on Homosexuality 1971* (Melbourne: Exacto Press).

Nelson, J., 1977, Apr 4, 'Homosexuality and the Church' *Christianity and Crisis*, 63-69.

Nicholi, A. M., 1993, 'Human Sexuality: A Psychiatric and Biblical Perspective', In Carson, D. A. & Woodbridge, J. D., *God and Culture: Essays in Honour of Carl F. H. Henry* (Grand Rapids: Eerdmans).

Nugent, R. and Gramick, J., 1989, 'Homosexuality: Protestant, Catholic and Jewish Issues; A Fishbone Tale', In R. Hasbany, ed., *Homosexuality and Religion* (New York and London: Haworth Press), 7-46.

Pattison, M. L., & Pattison, E. M., 'Ex-Gays: Religiously Mediated Change in Homosexuality', *American J Psychiatry* 137/12 (1980), 1553-1569.

Pittenger, N., 1976, *Time for Consent: A Christian's Approach to Homosexuality* (3rd ed; London: SCM).

Rekers, G., 1982, *Growing Up Straight: What Families Should Know About Homosexuality* (Chicago: Moody Press).

Remafedi et. al., 1992, 'Demography of Sexual Orientation in Adolescents', *Pediatrics* 89:714-721.

Rogers, S. M., Turner, C. F., 1991, 'Male-male sexual contact in the USA: Findings from five sample surveys, 1970-1990', *Journal of Sex Research* 28/4:491-519.

Salier, W. S., 1984, 'Homosexuality and the Biblical Norm', *Evangelical Journal* 2:77-95.

Scanzoni, L. and Mollenkott V. R., 1978, *Is the Homosexual My Neighbour? Another Christian View* (London: SCM).

Scroggs, R., 1983, *The New Testament and Homosexuality: Contextual Background for Contemporary Debate* (Philadelphia: Fortress Press).

Smith, A., 1991, 'The New Testament and Homosexuality', *Quarterly Review*, 11/4:18-32.

Smith, B. L., 1968, *Homosexuality and Abortion.* Based on addresses given to the Christian Medical Fellowship (Sydney).

Spong, J. S., 1988, *Living in Sin?* (San Fransisco: Harper & Row).

Ethics and Social Questions Committee, **(SSQC)**, 1973, *Report on Homosexuality: Report of the Ethics and Social Questions Committee to the Synod of the Church of England Diocese of Sydney* (Sydney: AIO).

Stafford, T., 1989, Aug, 'Coming Out', *Christianity Today* 33/11:16-21.

Stott, J. R. W., 1990, *Issues Facing Christians Today.* (2nd ed.; London: Collins Marshall Pickering), 336-364.

Sydney Synod, Diocese of, **(Sydney)**, 1981, *The Report of the Social Issues Sub-committee on Homosexuality.* Unpublished, undated paper.

_____, 1982a, *Comment on the Social Issues Sub Committee's Report on Male Homosexuality.* Unpublished, unsigned, undated paper.

_____, 1982b, *Report of the Standing Committee to the Second Session of the 39th Synod 1982.* Year Book of the Diocese of Sydney 1983 (Sydney: Diocesan Registry).

_____, 1985, *Report of the Standing Committee on a 1983 Synod Motion on Homosexuality and Ministry.*

Thielicke, H., 1962, *The Ethics of Sex.* Tr. J. W. Doberstein (New York: Harper and Row), 269-292.

Tiede, D. L., 1990, Spring, 'Will Idolaters, Sodomisers or the Greedy Inherit the Kingdom of God?' *Word and World* X/2:147-155.

Congregation for the Doctrine of the Faith, **(Vatican)**, 1986, *Letter to the Bishops of the Catholic Church on the Pastoral Care of Homosexual Persons;* Tr. Vatican Polyglot Press; (London: Catholic Truth Society).

Weltge, R. W., ed., 1969, *The Same Sex: An Appraisal of Homosexuality* (Philadelphia: Pilgrim Press).

Wenham, G.J., 1991, Sep, 'The Old Testament Attitude to Homosexuality', Expository Times 102/12: 359-363.

Williams, D., 1978, *The Bond That Breaks: Will Homosexuality Split the Church?* (Los Angeles: BIM).

Williams, M., 1993, 'Romans 1: Entropy, Sexuality and Politics', *Anvil* 10/2:105-110.

Williams, R., 1990, 'Toward a Theology for Lesbian and Gay Marriage' *Anglican Theological Review*, LXXII/2:134-157.

Wright, J. R., 1984, January, 'Boswell on Homosexuality: A Case Undemonstrated', *Anglican Theological Review* LXVI/1:79-94.

EXPLORING FURTHER

1. What is the precise meaning of 'homosexual'? Is it an either/or classification over against 'heterosexual' or is there a spectrum? If so, where on the spectrum does most of the 'heterosexual' population fit? Does it matter? In relation to sociology, it should be noted that in many Chinese, African and Pacific cultures (to name a few) homosexuality is unknown: does one conclude that it is a cultural, not a 'natural' phenomenon? Does the biblical witness justify support for the distinction between orientation and act?

2. What difference do varying theories of causation have on the pastoral approach to homosexual people? Should we

abandon attempts to work toward a 'cure' if we accept a 'nature' theory over against a 'nurture' theory?
3. What *range* of interpretations of biblical material on sexuality (and homosexuality in particular) are compatible with a reformed evangelical view of Scripture?

Regarding the choice between rejection and qualified acceptance, what does it boil down to? Is any love better than none? Is 'sexually handicapped' misleading? Why?
4. Should the fact that abstinent homosexuals have no potential for sexual fulfilment place them in a different category from heterosexual singles when it comes to making ethical decisions about the rightness of sexual activity?
5. What about 'homosexual covenants' in which two homosexually oriented Christians make a life-long vow to live together in celibacy? (Frame, 1989). Is it right? Is it wise? 'Proper expressions of sexuality for the single, the widowed, the married, the homosexual and the heterosexual are to be discovered and encouraged' (Cook, 1980, 304). Is this good advice? Should it be put into practice pastorally, and if so, how?

HOMOSEXUALITY IN SCRIPTURE

Barry G. Webb
Senior Lecturer in Old Testament, Moore College

Synopsis

Treatments of the biblical material relating to homosexuality have generally focussed on the few passages which make explicit reference to it. Terminology and background are subjected to intense scrutiny, often with little regard for the context in which the passages occur. The present paper seeks to move beyond this by relating these passages to the overarching themes of creation and redemption as they are progressively unfolded in Scripture as a whole. Homosexual practices are consistently condemned as contrary to God's will as expressed in creation, but hope is held out to homosexual and heterosexual sinners alike in the gospel of the coming Kingdom of God, centred on the person and work of Jesus Christ. The paper ends with some theological reflections on key issues in the current debate, with special reference to the foundational material of Genesis 1–3.

The brief I have been given is to set homosexuality in the context of God's purposes for us as men and women. The source material I am to draw on is Scripture (the Old and New Testaments), and the approach is to be that of Biblical Theology. This may seem straightforward enough, but there are a number of things that need clarification at the outset if we are not to end in frustrated expectations or outright confusion.

In the previous paper, Andrew Shead has noted that in recent theological discussion the term 'homosexuality' is generally taken to refer to an *orientation* towards members of the same sex, whether or not this is expressed in erotic sexual behaviour. This presents me with something of a dilemma, because it is now widely accepted that the biblical writers say nothing at all about homosexuality in this sense. They refer to homosexuals acts, but show no awareness of a distinct homosexual condition or orientation. So how shall we proceed? What I have chosen to do is to leave the question of orientation open and to begin with the question, 'What does Scripture say about erotic sexual activity between members of the same sex?' I'm prepared to go wherever the scriptural data leads me, but this is my starting point.

But this brings us at once to another issue. To expect Scripture to 'say' something assumes that in some sense it is a coherent whole; that either it speaks with one voice or that its various voices are, in the last analysis, complementary rather than contradictory. This paper assumes that Scripture does indeed have such coherence and that the key to its coherence is Jesus Christ. I take seriously the claim of the Gospel writers that Jesus quoted the Old Testament as the Word of God and maintained that it found its fulfilment in him (Matt 22:31; Luke 24:25-27, 44-45). I also take seriously the claim that the apostles (including Paul) were directly commissioned by Christ and that their teaching is fundamentally one with his (John 16:12-15; Gal 1:1, 11-24). The coherence of Scripture is grounded ultimately in the speaking activity of God: 'In many and various ways God has spoken of old to our fathers through the prophets; but in these last days he has spoken to us by a Son ...' (Heb 1:1-2). And God's speaking in Jesus cannot be divorced from his speaking in Scripture. Unless we are prepared to invent our own Christ we must have the one that Scripture delivers to us, and note carefully his words in Matt 22:31: 'Have you not read what was spoken to you by God?' (citing Exod 3:6). Jesus is our key to Scripture as he is to everything else. The implication of this is that in engaging with Scripture we engage with the mind of God, the God who has revealed himself finally in Jesus Christ. To ask what Scripture says about a topic is to ask what God has said about it. And if this is true, it follows that what Scripture says about a topic must control all subsequent deliberations about it by the believing community.

So our aim is to engage with the mind of God in Scripture. But Scripture as it has come to us has a definite shape to it. It moves from creation, through Fall and redemption, to new creation. There is beginning and end; there is promise and fulfilment; there is inauguration and completion; there is complication and resolution, and movement towards a goal. And again, Jesus is key to this whole dynamic structure. He is the link between the Old and New Testaments because in him the Old Covenant is fulfilled and the New inaugurated. And the end towards which everything moves is the unveiling, the revelation of the full effects of what God has achieved in Christ (Rev 1:4-8). The approach of this paper is that of 'biblical theology' in that it takes this shape of the Bible's theology as given and works with it. The aim is to see in what contexts homosexuality first appears in the progressive unfolding of the biblical revelation, what perspectives are developed on it, how these are nuanced by the fulfilment that comes in Christ, and by the vision of the new heavens and the new earth to which the whole biblical revelation finally moves.

This means, among other things, that we will need to be attentive to the Bible's own internal hermeneutic. Options which may seem equally valid from reading, say, the Genesis material, will be subject to review and sifting in the light of what we find in the Law or the Prophets, and further still by what we find in the Gospels and the Epistles. The teaching of Jesus, in particular, will have a privileged status because of his key significance within the total structure. And we will expect the eschaton, as Jesus and the apostles teach about it and as the book of Revelation describes it, to provide us with the final perspective that should inform our present behaviour. Because of its recognition of the key significance of Jesus Christ for the Bible's total message, Biblical Theology ideally yields a thoroughly Christian appropriation of Scripture, including the Old Testament.

It is clear from all this where we must start, namely, with the foundational material of Genesis 1-3, and in particular with the treatment of human sexuality in these chapters. This is so for several reasons. First, Biblical Theology, to be truly such, must begin where the Bible itself begins. For us this will not be an absolute beginning because we have already read the rest of the Bible and know where it is going. We already know the plot, so to speak, at least in outline. But our interest here is not in the main plot as such, but in how a particular issue, homosexuality, is related to the main plot. And we will surely not have a sufficiently clear idea of this unless we have read from the beginning with this particular issue in mind. We also have to begin at the beginning because our chosen method is essentially exegetical. As we have seen in the previous paper there are only a limited number of texts which explicitly refer to homosexuality. But our aim here is not to use these as proof-texts. Our method demands, instead, that we read up to them and beyond them, noting how they contribute to the broader flow of the biblical message at the points where they occur. That again means that we must begin where the canon begins. And finally, we must begin here because, although Genesis 1–3 does not speak of homosexuality as such, it lays the groundwork for what will be said about it later.

In the beginning: human sexuality in God's creative purposes

Genesis begins with two complementary accounts of creation. The first (1:1 – 2:3) describes creation in six successive days leading to the rest of the seventh day. The creation of man (human beings) in the image of God, is the crowning act of creation. In the second (2:4-25), the focus is on the man Adam, and his relationship to the earth and to his environment. Particular stress is placed on his aloneness, and his need of a suitable companion. This account climaxes with the creation of Eve and the union of Adam and Eve in marriage.

Clearly each account has its own distinctive character. Even the order in which things happen differs in the two accounts. In the first, vegetation (grass, trees, and so on) are created before the creation of man. In the second they are created afterwards. But this apparently was no problem to the author of Genesis, nor to the those who transmitted it to us as Holy Scripture. They apparently regarded both these ancient stories as true in their own way, and as complementing rather than contradicting each other. That's why they are simply placed side-by-side at the beginning of the Bible. We need both of them to get the full message about creation that the writer wants to give us.

So let's leave the chronology to one side for a moment and try to understand the messages the two accounts deliver about God and man, and how they are related to one another and to the world. In the first account God simply speaks and the world (including man) comes into existence. He is above and beyond the world, and his word has absolute power. This account focuses on his transcendence. In the second account God is like a gardener and a potter. He plants a garden, fashions man out of the soil and breathes life into him. God is still in control here, but he is down to earth, deeply and intimately involved with his world. This account stresses his immanence. The two accounts together tell us that God is both transcendent and immanent; above and beyond his creation, and deeply involved with it.

The two accounts deliver a similar message about man and his relationship to the world. In chapter 1 he is made in the image of God, and appointed ruler of the world by God. But in chapter 2 he is made from the dust, intimately connected with the land and the animals. Man is both lord of his environment and deeply dependent on it. He is related both to God, who is above him, and the animals, who are below him. He is a creature of great dignity and frailty.

The point is that we need both the accounts to give us the full picture of both God and man and their relationship to one another and to the world. At the level of theme or message, the two stories clearly complement rather than contradict one another. The fact that we cannot construct an exact chronology of creation from them is beside the point; it was not the writer's purpose to give us that kind of information.

And now, if we focus particularly on the way human sexuality is portrayed in the two accounts we will notice a similar complementarity. In the first account, man (humankind) is made in the image of God and given the mandate to rule the earth. But this general statement is immediately followed by the more particular statements: 'male and female he created them ... and said to them, "Be fruitful and multiply, and fill the earth and subdue it"'. Human beings will be able to rule the earth only if they can reproduce themselves and establish their presence everywhere. In this account, the purpose of the male/female distinction within the human race is reproduction.

The situation in the second account is quite different. Here the man, created first, is given a far more limited task. He is placed in the garden to till it and keep it (v.15). There is no suggestion that the task is beyond him, or unpleasant in itself. It is only after the Fall that such work becomes arduous. The problem is the aloneness of the man, and it is this to which our attention is pointedly drawn by the 'not good' of v.18 (contrast the divine pronouncements of chapter 1). The woman is then created precisely to remedy this condition of aloneness. She will be a helper to the man by sharing his work in the garden, but far more importantly, by sharing his life, by being a companion who will remedy his aloneness. The climax is reached, to be sure, in the one flesh union of the happy pair (v.24), but if the passage as a whole is taken into account, this is an end in itself, not a means to an end. The purpose of the man/woman complementarity here is companionship, the sharing of life and work, the removal of aloneness, rather than reproduction as such. That is at best incidental to the main purpose of their relationship.

Taken together the two accounts deliver the message that the divine purpose of the male-female polarity within the human race is *both* reproduction *and* companionship. And antecedent to both of these is the dignity inherent in being made in the image of God, a dignity shared by all human beings irrespective of their sex.

Of course, a host of difficult questions emerge at this point, many of them with particular relevance for our topic. The first relates to genre. Clearly what we are dealing with at one level is aetiologies, stories about origins. But are they more than this? Does the fact that God commanded the first pair to reproduce mean that all couples are bound to do so? And is 2:24 purely descriptive ('Therefore a man leaves his father and mother and cleaves to his wife') or is there an implied command ('... will leave ...')?

And more fundamentally, what is the relationship between the world of Genesis 1–2 and our world, and between the teaching of these chapters and Christian obligation today? Genesis 1–2 envisages an ideal world in which every man has his female companion. But what happens when, for whatever reason, this is not possible? Are there other remedies for the loneliness of a man which are not envisaged here but are legitimate in the changed situation brought about by the Fall? And what about the loneliness of a woman?

None of these questions can be resolved decisively by subjecting these chapters to more intense scrutiny, although this may help. The fundamental solution to all of them is to read on. Certainly Genesis 1–2 envisages development beyond what is actually realised there. The command to 'fill the earth and subdue it' places the whole progress of civilisation with its arts and sciences potentially under the rubric of divine blessing. And the command to reproduce entails the development of ever more varied and complex human relationships as human society expands. The question before us in this paper is whether the emergence of homosexual relationships may be seen as a natural or necessary development of the given situation which we have at the beginning.

The Fall: relationships distorted

The fundamental move from the ideal world of Genesis 1–2 to the world as we now experience it is made with the biblical account of the Fall in Genesis 3. After the teaching about the original created order comes an analysis, in chapter 3, of what has gone wrong with it. Again the message is delivered in story form, and what it boils down to is that man has allowed his own desires to rule his life instead of God. He has used the power to choose, which God gave him, to rebel against his maker—to make a god of himself. And he has been encouraged in this course by a being who has already chosen that path before him, represented in the story by the serpent. The chapter ends by telling how, as a result of this choice, man began to experience something new in his relationship with God—judgment. But notice, not only judgment. God thrusts the human pair out of the garden, but confirms his continued care for them by clothing them (v.21). Now, however, they will have to make their way in a world where struggle, pain and suffering will be a daily reminder of the fact that all is not well between them and their maker.

Again, there are many questions this story does not answer. If the world created by God was good, how is an evil creature (the serpent) within it? How can a serpent talk? Are we meant to take the serpent literally, or is it a symbol for something? If so, what? And what precisely is signified by the tree of the knowledge of good and evil? The story answers none of these questions, intriguing though they are. It really answers only one: What has gone wrong with the world? And the answer is crystal clear: the human race has rebelled against God. And it traces that rebellion to its root: pride ('You will be as gods ...'). Everything else is irrelevant to the writer. That is the message he wants to deliver, and the account he has given delivers it with devastating clarity.

Chapters 4–11 unfold the full impact of that original act of rebellion. Now that the most fundamental relationship of all has been fractured (man's relationship with God) all other relationships begin to fall apart as well. Even religion becomes a source of human rivalry and murderous jealousy. Brother kills brother, violence and immorality fill the earth, and finally, in the account of the tower of Babel of chapter 11, a humanistic civilisation emerges whose very first principle is defiance of God.

It now becomes clear that the Fall, too, points beyond itself to much else. The original act of rebellion was singular and uncomplicated: the host of evils that follow it are complex and various. But they all grow from the original act as from a single seed, and they all receive the same basic response from God: judgment, tempered with mercy. A protective mark is placed on Cain; Noah is told to build a boat. Only in the last episode, the tower of Babel, is no mercy evident. Human society is thrown into utter confusion and scattered over the face of the earth. A terrible silence hangs over the scene. It seems like the end. The human race has reaped the full reward of its rebellion. God has withdrawn; judgment has been his final word. But no, a new movement begins in ch.12, as grace breaks through again in the call of Abraham: 'in you all families of the earth shall be blessed' (12:3).

It is now plain that not everything that follows after the original created order of Genesis 1–2 can be seen as legitimate or approved developments from it. The act of rebellion in chapter 3 gives rise to a whole new category of human activities which come under the general rubric of rebellion against God. And a consistent pattern of divine response to such acts is beginning to emerge: judgment, tempered with mercy. Homosexuality has not yet appeared, but there are now two potential categories into which it could fall.

But before going further we must pause to reflect more closely on the impact of the Fall on the relationship between the original human pair. In the pronouncement of judgment following their disobedience their relationship is described in terms of desire (תְּשׁוּקָה) on her part, and rule (מָשַׁל) on his. The terminology itself does not have any necessarily negative connotations. מָשַׁל, for example, has been used in chapter 1 of the beneficent and life-giving rule of the sun and moon (1:16). But the context here in chapter 3 strongly suggests that something less positive is on view. The desire and rule language comes in a judgment speech, immediately preceded by pain, and followed by thorns and thistles. At the very least, something less seems to be on view here then the rapturous oneness of the pair at the end of chapter 2. More ominously still, what is said here anticipates the recurrence of the same terminology in 4:7, where Yahweh is warning Cain about the consequences of his anger:

> If you do not do well, sin is crouching at the door; its desire (תְּשׁוּקָתוֹ) is for you, but you must master it (מָשַׁל).

We know the result. Instead of mastering his sinful desire he was mastered by it, and the result was a total breakdown in his relationship with Abel, leading to death.

It is clear from this that Genesis draws a sharp distinction between pre-Fall and post-Fall relationships. The former are part of the good, created order of things. The latter are part of the disordered state of affairs resulting from human disobedience and divine judgment. Disorder in relationships, including sexual relationships, results from the refusal of human beings to live according to the limits and permissions given by God.

The Fall produces disorder in sexual relationships. Neither the desiring of the woman nor the ruling of the man is wholly good; their companionship is now marred by conflict. The woman still knows herself to be a woman and the man knows himself to be a man. They are conscious of their nakedness (3:7). The man and the woman each retain their sexual identity as God created it. But the way they express it is no longer wholly good, as it had been before the Fall.

Sodom: all boundaries crossed

It is not until Genesis 19 (the rescue of Lot from Sodom) that we first encounter homosexual behaviour directly. This must, of course, be understood against the backdrop of the earlier chapters. But first to the details of the passage itself, and since they are so similar to those of Judges 19 (the Levite and his concubine in Gibeah) we will deal with both passages at this point.

In the first, Lot entertains two angels in Sodom. From the way they are greeted and referred to we must assume that they have the form of adult males. At night the men of Sodom gather outside Lot's house and noisily demand that he bring his guests out to them so that they may 'know them'. Lot is shocked at this affront to his guests. He offers to give them his two virgin daughters instead, but the offer is refused. The men of Sodom are angered by this attempt by Lot, a mere sojourner, to 'play the judge' by meddling in their affairs. They attempt to force their way into the house but are prevented from doing so by Lot's guests, who strike them with blindness.

In Judges 19 a Levite and his concubine, who are staying overnight in Gibeah, are entertained by an old man who is himself a temporary resident. When confronted with the same demand as Lot, this host offers the men outside his own virgin daughter and his guest's concubine. They refuse the offer, but when the Levite thrusts his concubine out anyway, they 'know her' and abuse her all night, leaving her all but dead.

In his influential book published in 1955, D. Sherwin Bailey denied that the verb 'know' (יָדַע) in the initial demand in these narratives had any sexual connotation.[1] He found only fifteen examples of 'know' in this sense in the Old Testament, against more than nine hundred in its primary, non-sexual sense, and argued that the context in both passages fully justified the normal, common meaning of the word. The host in both narratives is a foreigner who has just received other foreigners without consulting the local inhabitants. They are demanding to know who these strangers are, and the host is protesting against the discourtesy to his guests which such a demand involves. The sin of the men in the street is boorish hostility to foreigners rather than sexual perversion. In the incident recorded in Judges they do later engage in perverted sex, but it is heterosexual rather than homosexual.

In reply, Derek Kidner has rightly pointed out that the statistical argument carries little weight. If matters such as this could be settled by statistics the rarer sense of a word would *never* seem probable.[2] It is the context which must decide the issue. And the disputed word 'know', certainly *is* subsequently used in its sexual sense in both stories. In Genesis 19:8 the host has two daughters who have not 'known' man, and in Judges 19:25 the men in the street 'know' the Levite's concubine. This does not require that 'know' have the same meaning at every point; there could be a deliberate play on it. But it certainly calls Bailey's argument into serious question. The host, in both stories, apparently understands the demand to be for sexual gratification. But, against Kidner, it is strange that the homosexuals in the second narrative (if that is what they are) behave like

---

[1] *Homosexuality and the Western Christian Tradition* (Hamden: Shoestring Press).

[2] D. Kidner, *Genesis. An Introduction and Commentary* (Tyndale Old Testament Commentaries; London: Tyndale Press, 1967), 137.

heterosexuals when given the opportunity to do so. The fact of the matter is that there are problems with both the proposed readings.

For Kidner, the matter is clinched by the reference to Genesis 19 in Jude 7: 'Sodom and Gomorrah and the surrounding cities ... acted immorally and indulged in unnatural lust'. In terms of the general approach of this paper appeal to a relevant NT passage in these circumstances is quite legitimate. But the precise meaning of the verse in question is not clear enough to be decisive. The previous verse, which refers to 'the angels that did not keep their proper position' is almost certainly an allusion to the passage in Genesis 6:1-4 about illicit relationships between the sons of God and the daughters of men. That passage, too, is a thorny one. But Codex Alexandrinus has 'angels of God', and early Jewish and Christian commentators agree that what is on view is a transgression of the boundary between the divine and human realms, angels consorting with human beings.[3] It is this traditional interpretation which is reflected in Jude 6 (cf. 2 Pet 2:4-6; 1 Pet 3:19-20). This being so, the 'unnatural lust' of verse 7 (literally 'going after strange flesh') probably refers, not to homosexuality in particular, but to the fact that 'the sin of the men of Sodom ... reached its peak when they sought intercourse with the angels sent to Lot'.[4] The issue is not homosexuality as such, but a general state of immorality, both homosexual and heterosexual, which reached such extremes that it threatened to transgress the boundary between the human and the divine, as in the days before the Flood[5]. In short, there can be no simple equation drawn between the 'unnatural lust' of Jude 7 and homosexuality, and consequently appeal to this verse does not settle the issue

---

[3] Kidner, 84.
[4] D. H. Wheaton, 'Jude', Guthrie and others, eds, *The New Bible Commentary Revised* London: IVP, 1970), 1276.
[5] Though in the reverse direction.

in the way Kidner thinks it does. Homosexuality per se is not the primary issue in either of the two OT narratives in question. On the traditional and most probable reading of them, the demand to 'know' the visitors in both cases is a demand for sex. But the general atmosphere of violence suggests that, if we are to narrow our focus to the sexual-behaviour aspect of each narrative, the perversion involved is rape rather than homosexuality.[6] And if homosexual rape is condemned in the first passage, heterosexual rape is far more clearly condemned in the second. In short there *is* an allusion to homosexual behaviour in these two passages, and it occurs in a context of judgment on human sin. But exegesis does *not* indicate that homosexuality per se is the issue. What is condemned is demanding to 'know' people, actually 'knowing' them, or handing them over to others to be so 'known', without their consent. It is the sin of using people sexually without regard for their dignity as human beings.

But now that we have grasped the exegetical nettle it is time for some more general observations.

First, the sexual sin of the Sodomites is part of a more general state of disorder, including inhospitality, xenophobia, and violence. 2 Pet 2:7-8 sums it up as licentiousness and lawlessness (RSV). We have focussed on the sexual aspect only because of the terms of reference of our study.

Second, in its canonical context the sin of Sodom falls against the backdrop of Genesis 3. It is a further outworking of the disorder in human relationships that results from human rebellion against God. It has its root in the Fall and in its most extreme form is an assault on God himself, represented in the story by his two messengers.

Third, it is not the sin of pagans only, but also of the people of God, as the parallel in Judges 19 makes very clear. For the place involved there is 'Gibeah of Benjamin', an Israelite town. The same point is made more subtly in Genesis. Lot may be better than the people of Sodom (2 Pet

---

[6] Recent studies have suggested, probably correctly, that the offending men in both stories were fundamentally heterosexual, but their object was to humiliate the foreigners by subjecting them to homosexual rape, as was often done to prisoners of war in the ancient world.

2:8 calls him a 'righteous man'), but he is not untainted by their sin, especially in the final stages of his stay there. If we read the account carefully we will see that not only is Lot in Sodom but Sodom is in Lot. Under pressure, he offers his own virgin daughters to the men of Sodom, and he himself is eventually sexually abused by those same daughters (19:8, 30-38). He leaves Sodom, but takes its sin with him. The fact is (to use NT terminology) that the sin of Sodom is in the church as well as in the world.

Fourth, the sin of Sodom meets with the same response from God here as we have seen earlier in Genesis: judgment (the overthrow of the city) tempered with mercy (the rescue of Lot). But the judgment here is so catastrophic that, along with the Flood, it becomes a paradigm of divine retribution for generations to come (see Isa 1:9-10; Hag 2:21-22). And in the longer perspective of the Bible's theology it is an anticipation of the final judgment (Jude 7). God has served notice on the world (both pagans and his own people) that such behaviour will not go unpunished. In Judges 19-20 it is punished by a civil war in which the whole of Israel suffers, and the Benjamites in particular are 'handed over' by Yahweh to be virtually wiped out by the other tribes (20:28-48).

Finally, if homosexuality as such is not the issue in these passages it does not follow that they approve of it, still less that Scripture as a whole does. Our inquiry is far from over yet. What it does mean is that we should not use these passages as proof-texts against homosexuals and fail to see their relevance to heterosexuals.

Sexual taboos: Leviticus 18:22; 20:13

With Leviticus we move from narrative to material that is directly prescriptive. We now find ourselves in the world of command and prohibition. The 'statutes' of the pagan nations (18:3) are set in stark contrast to the 'statutes and ordinances' of Yahweh (18:4-5), which are collectively his 'charge' to Israel (18:30). The same terminology is used in chapter 20 (vv.8, 22, 23).[7] To fail to keep Yahweh's charge is to 'defile' both oneself and the land (18:20, 28), and to 'profane' Yahweh's name (18:21), by committing 'abomination' (18:22), 'perversion' (18:23) and 'wickedness' (20:14). The penalty is to be put to death (by stoning or burning), and to be cut off from the community by Yahweh (20:2-3, 5, 6, 9-16). It is in this context that we find the two prohibitions of 18:22 and 20:13.

> You shall not lie with a male as with a woman; it is an abomination.

> If a man lies with a male as with a woman, both of them have committed an abomination; they shall be put to death, their blood is upon them.

Although it is disputed, there can be little doubt that this is a general proscription of homosexual intercourse. The only serious objection, as indicated in the previous paper, maintains that the term 'abomination' (תּוֹעֵבָה) is a cultic term, and therefore it is cult prostitution rather than homosexual intercourse of the common kind that is on view. But while 'abomination' is commonly used of cultic offences, especially in Deuteronomy and Ezekiel, it is also used of non-cultic offences, as frequently in Proverbs. And in Leviticus itself it is not used at all outside chapters 18 and 20—the very passages in question. So there is no established cultic usage in Leviticus to constrain our reading. The matter must be settled contextually, and on that basis the ordinary, non-cultic sense is strongly indicated. The single, blanket prohibition against homosexual intercourse in 18:22 is the counterpart to the whole string of heterosexual taboos which have preceded it, none of which suggests a cultic context (not with your mother, not with your sister, not with your grand-daughter, and so on). The fact that no such specifics are given for homosexual relationships makes it clear that it is homosexuality as a whole that is being proscribed. Specification is superfluous. The situation is the same in chapter 20. The only clearly cultic prohibition is against offering children to Molech (v.21; cf. 20:1-5). But this is

---

[7] 'Customs' in the RSV of 20:23 is the same as word as 'statutes' in 18:3.

probably included here precisely because of the moral outrage that it involved; the children were almost certainly burnt.[8] The language of defilement in verses 27-28, to be sure, has cultic connotations. The land is Yahweh's sanctuary; if it is defiled it will no longer be a fit place for him to dwell with his people. But the previous use of the same language in connection with adultery in the same passage (v.22) makes it clear that it is moral rather than cultic defilement that is primarily on view. The defilement of the land here results from the moral defilement of its inhabitants.

Homosexuality, then, is a moral issue in Leviticus, along with incest and adultery. In this respect chapters 18-20 in general contrast sharply with chapters 11-15 where the commands and prohibitions relate entirely to matters of ceremonial purity: clean and unclean foods, the ceremonial purification of women after childbirth, the cleansing of lepers, and instructions regarding bodily emissions. Cultic and ceremonial matters come to the fore again in chapters 21 and following, but in chapters 18-20 the focus lies elsewhere.

The reason given for the prohibitions of chapter 18 is simply that the specified acts are abhorrent to Yahweh ('abominations' is his word for them). It is because the former inhabitants of Canaan practised such things that Yahweh punished them by driving them out (v.24). To explain the prohibition against homosexuality in terms of a state of paranoia on the part of the author regarding all things Canaanite is to simply ignore (or still worse, dismiss out of hand) the theology of the text. The biblical writers in fact suggest that Israelites in general were strongly attracted to Canaanite ways; the divine prohibition cut across their natural inclinations. The positive motivation for the prohibition is given in the opening and closing words of the larger unit in which they occur: 'I am Yahweh your God' (18:2); 'You shall be holy ... for I Yahweh am holy' (20:26). Israel is in covenant with Yahweh, and must reflect his character in her relationships. Abstinence from things which are abhorrent to

---

[8] For a thorough discussion see J. E. Hartley, *Leviticus* (Word Commentary; Dallas: Word, 1992), 333-337.

Yahweh is a necessary expression of her relationship with him.

This already points us to a much larger theological context. But in order to appreciate it fully we need to pause at this point to note the special contribution of chapter 20. Here, basically, the same catalogue of prohibitions occur as in chapter 18, but this time with the penalty specified, which in most cases, including homosexual intercourse, is death (20:1-16, 18). Chapter 20 forces us to grapple with the theology of retribution in Leviticus, and especially the theology behind the death penalty.

The broad concern of Leviticus is with how the covenant relationship between Yahweh and Israel which has been given formal expression in the Sinai Covenant (Exod 19–24) is to be maintained, given the frailty and sinfulness of Israel. The answer is fundamentally by the mercy of God expressed in the sacrificial system: 'the life of the flesh is in the blood; and I [Yahweh] have given it for you upon the altar to make atonement for your souls' (17:11). The general principle is that all sin deserves death. The one who sins against Yahweh forfeits his life. But Yahweh in his mercy will accept the life of a sacrificial animal in place of the life of the sinner. So in Yahweh's dealings with his people the accent falls on mercy rather than judgment. Unwitting sins are provided for in the sacrificial system (4:2, 13). But deliberate sin places the offender beyond the reach of this provision, and therefore subject to the death sentence. This is implicit in Leviticus, as the language of 4:2, 13 ('sins unwittingly') makes clear. It is spelled out quite explicitly in Numbers 15:27-30. Against this background it appears that the offences listed in Leviticus 18 and 20 were deemed to be deliberate by their very nature and therefore required the death penalty. But as the test case given in 19:21-22 makes clear, care was taken to protect the innocent in cases involving special circumstances.

But the ultimate ground for the death penalty lies in the Creation/Fall material of Genesis. Death is first threatened (2:17) and then imposed (3:19) by God as the ultimate sanction against human rebellion. The general principle is that those who rebel against God forfeit their lives. The sentence is universal and put into effect by God himself. But after the Flood, for the first time, this is brought into the arena of human judicial responsibility: 'Whoever sheds the blood of man, by man shall his blood be shed; for God made man in his own image' (Gn. 9:6). Murder is a capital offence because it is a direct assault on the created order established by God, in which man, made in his image, functions as his representative. In their canonical context the prohibitions and penalties of Leviticus 18 and 20 move against this background as their raison d'etre. And so once again we are driven back to the foundational material of Genesis 1-3. The Sinai Covenant must be seen as a particular expression of the relationship between God and the world implicit in creation itself, and incest, adultery and homosexuality as violations of the created order.

And with this we have virtually exhausted the relevant OT material. Given the acknowledged fertility orientation of Canaanite religious rites, the 'male cult prostitutes' (RSV, Heb. קָדֵשׁ) of 1 Kings 14:24; 15:12; 22:46, and 2 Kings 23:7 (cf. Deut 23:17) were probably used by women rather than men, and in any case, there is nothing in these passages to offset in any way the general strictures of Leviticus.[9]

The Gospels: the dawn of a new era

The Gospels form the bridge between the Old and New Testaments. Because of this they are crucial to our topic, even

---

[9] The probitition of men wearing women's clothing and vice verse (Dt 22:5) points in the same direction. Cases have been made out, some much more plausible than others, that certain well-known biblical characters had homosexual relationships: David and Jonothan, Ruth and Naomi, and in the NT, Paul and Timothy, and even Jesus and John (the 'beloved' disciple). For perhaps the most scholarly example of such writing, see T. Horner, *Jonathan Loved David. Homosexuality in Biblical Times* (Philadelphia: The Westminster Press, 1978), chs 1-3. Although Horner makes out a plausible case for an affair between David and Jonathan, it rests mainly on extra-biblical parallels, textual emendations, and reading between the lines. And even if the case for such an affair could be proved, it would not sigificantly affect the general stance which Scripture as a whole takes towards homosexual behaviour.

though, paradoxically, they contain no direct reference to homosexuality. It is in the Gospels that the new, Christian era is inaugurated in the life, death and resurrection of Jesus Christ. What we have here is fundamental to the way we are to both appropriate what has gone before and approach what is to come. In particular, what we are to do with the Leviticus material depends foundationally on what the Gospels have to say concerning Jesus and his attitude to the Mosaic law.

An obvious starting point is Matt 5:17: Jesus did not come to abolish the law and the prophets but to fulfil them. The key word, 'fulfil' ($\pi\lambda\eta\rho\delta\omega$), may mean, among other things, to accomplish, to obey, to bring out the full meaning, to complete by bringing to a goal. In Matthew it is most commonly used of bringing to realisation something that was promised.[10] This sense is reinforced here by reference to the prophets. But 'the law and the prophets' is a regular Jewish expression for the OT as a whole (cf. 7:12; 22:40; Acts 24:14; 28:23; Rom 3:21). So the point is that the whole of the OT, the law as well as the prophets, pointed forward to what Jesus now brings into being. To see precisely how he does this we have to read on.

Jesus fulfils the law in his teaching. He not only upholds the commandments relating to murder, adultery, divorce, false witness, retribution, and love of neighbour, but insists that they may be broken as much by wrong attitudes as by wrong acts (Matt 5:21-47). The food laws he effectively abrogates, but only to expose the deeper issues of cleanness and defilement of which they were shadows (Matt 15:15-20; Mark 7:14-23; cf. Matt 5:8). He treats the Sabbath with a freedom that shocks the rigorists of his day (Matt 12:1-14), but only after he has invited them to find in him their true rest (11:28-30). In short, Jesus intensifies the moral dimension of the law. As for its ceremonial aspects, he exposes the moral and spiritual realities to which they point and demands response to these as the true form of obedience. And he summarises his teaching about the law with an absolute demand ('Be perfect, as your heavenly Father is perfect', Matt 5:48) and a concise

---

[10] See the discussion in R.T. France, *The Gospel According to Matthew* (Tyndale Commentary; Leicester: IVP, 1985), 38-40.

summary (Love God and love your neighbour; 'on these two commandments depend all the law and the prophets', Matt 22:36-40).

Second, Jesus fulfils the law in his living. He himself embodies the perfection which mirrors that of the Father. And as for love of neighbour, he regards all people, regardless of their sinfulness or social standing, as potential candidates for inclusion in the kingdom of heaven. He is the friend of publicans and sinners. There are no untouchables for him. In fact his most stringent criticisms are of the self-righteous and hypocritical who withhold love from such people. At the same time, however, he calls for repentance. This call is fundamental to his preaching and is directed to all alike (Mark 1:15). Even those he refuses to condemn he urges not to sin again (John 8:11; cf. 5:14).

Finally, Jesus fulfils the law by his death. As 'the Lamb of God who takes away the sin of the world' (John 1:29) he is the final and perfect sacrifice which makes further atonement unnecessary. By taking the death penalty himself he ransoms others (Matt 20:28; Mark 10:45). By his death he inaugurates the new covenant (Luke 22:20; cf. Matt 26:28; Mark 14:24) which makes permanent, universal forgiveness possible (Luke 24:47). The only sin which now places the one who commits it beyond the reach of forgiveness is the refusal to accept what is offered (John 3:16-36). In Jesus both the mercy and judgment aspects of the law reach their goal. He is God's full provision and his final offer.

With this framework we may now give our attention to some aspects of Jesus' teaching which have more particular relevance to our topic.

Given that, in general, Jesus' teaching on sexual matters is more stringent than that of the Mosaic law, the lack of any explicit mention of homosexual behaviour can hardly be taken as an implicit endorsement of it. The prohibition against it in the law belongs to the same category of commandments (moral) that he repeated and intensified rather than those (the ceremonial) which he abrogated. It stands in close proximity to the prohibition against adultery in both chapter 18 and chapter 20 of Leviticus (18:20, 22; 20:10, 13).

Further, in his teaching on divorce Jesus points to Genesis 2 as normative. The Mosaic law made concessions because of hardness of heart, 'but from the beginning it was not so' (Matt 19:8). This confirms that the Mosaic legislation was intended, in general, to reflect the created order as represented in Genesis 2 and to prevent violations of it. Jesus' teaching gives fresh expression to this basic principle.

There is an intriguing reference in Matt 19:12 to eunuchs 'who have been so from birth'. The context is Jesus' quotation of Gen 2:24: 'For this reason a man shall leave his father and mother and be joined to his wife' (v.5). The disciples object that if divorce is to be ruled out in the new order of things which Jesus is bringing in, then it is better not to marry (v.10). Jesus responds that, in general, marriage is God's intention for people, but there are exceptions: this 'word' concerning marriage cannot be received by all, 'but only those to whom it is given' (v.12). He then proceeds to list those to whom it is *not* given. In general, it is not given to eunuchs, but these are of three kinds: those who have been eunuchs from birth, those who have been made so by men, and those (like Jesus himself) who have, so to speak, made themselves eunuchs for the sake of the kingdom of God. The first two groups are incapable of marriage; the third group have voluntarily renounced it.

Several things need to be noted here. 'Eunuchs from birth' refers to a condition for which the person concerned is not responsible. Comparison with 'eunuchs who have been made so by men' suggests that it is essentially a physical condition which is on view, though it would inevitably have secondary psychological aspects. And it would appear to involve an incapacity for sexual intercourse as such rather than an orientation towards same-sex intercourse. It is unlikely, therefore, that there is any reference here to homosexuality as a congenital condition. Finally, although the tone of the passage is clearly sympathetic to the plight of the eunuch[11], the only alternatives entertained are heterosexual marriage or sexual abstinence, by either necessity or choice.

But what hope, then, does Jesus offer to those to whom the satisfactions of marriage are not given? The first is that, provided they have made themselves ready by believing the gospel, they will be included in the final marriage between Christ and his people (Matt 25:1-3; cf. 9:14-15). And second, that in the entirely new order of things that will then come into existence, they will experience a quality of relationships that will utterly transcend what they have missed out on in this life; for 'those who are accounted worthy to attain that age and to the resurrection of the dead neither marry nor are given in marriage ... for they are equal to the angels and are the sons of God' (Luke 20:35-36). Paradoxically, the final marriage will totally obliterate the distinctions that have previously existed between participants and abstainers, the married and the unmarried. In terms of Biblical Theology, we begin with a marriage between a man and a woman, and we end with the marriage between Christ and his church. The end is not a return to the beginning, but a movement to something which transcends it (Rev 9:6-10).

In the Gospels, then, we catch a glimpse of the end to which the biblical revelation is moving, but we are not quite there. The epistles have yet to spell out the full implications of the gospel for Christian living.

The Epistles: life in the last days

In Romans 1 Paul is laying the foundations for his generalisations in chapter 3: 'all men ... are under the power of sin', and 'all have sinned and fall short of the glory of God' (vv.9, 23). He is establishing the guilt of all only that, having done so, he may then go on to speak of the justification that is available to all as a gift 'through the redemption that is in Christ Jesus' (3:24). More particularly, from 1:18 onwards,

---

[11] Cf. Isaiah 56:3-5. The 'eunuch' was probably a social outcast in both Jesus' world and the world addressed by Isaiah 56.

Paul is intent on showing how 'the wrath of God is revealed from heaven against all ungodliness and wickedness of men', that is, how God, even now, displays his anger by judging sinners in observable ways. The fundamental way is by giving them up to dishonourable passions (v.26). The past tense of verses 24, 26 and 28 ('gave them up') is best understood in relation to the individuals concerned ('those who do such things', v.32). Such people show by the very extent of their depravity that the restraining hand of God has been removed from them. Paradoxically he has judged them by giving them over into the grip of the things they themselves have chosen—things which are destructive by their very nature. Hence they receive 'in their own persons the due penalty of their deeds' (v.27). It is in this context that reference is made to homosexuality:

> Their women exchanged natural relations for unnatural, and the men likewise gave up natural relations with women and were consumed with passion for one another, men committing shameless acts with men ... (vv. 26-27).

Erotic sexual activity is being referred to. The acts are same-sex and passionate, and for the first time we have female as well as male homosexuality on view. This much is clear. But certain expressions require comment.

The activities involved are said to be 'unnatural' ($\pi\alpha\rho\grave{\alpha}$ $\phi\acute{u}\sigma\iota\nu$, v.26). These are contrasted in this verse and the next with opposite gender sexual relations, which are said to be 'natural' ($\phi\nu\sigma\iota\kappa\acute{\eta}$). And the whole discussion moves against the references to creation in verse 20 ('the creation of the world ... the things that have been made'). So $\phi\acute{u}\sigma\iota\varsigma$, 'nature', in this context clearly denotes the world as God has made it, the created order. Paul has something more in mind than custom. He is appealing to what, in terms of the Bible's own theology, is prior to all culture: the will of God for human relationships expressed in the way he made us 'from the beginning' (Matt 19:4). Again we are back at Genesis 1-2.

But what of the verbs 'exchanged' ($\mu\epsilon\tau\alpha\lambda\lambda\acute{\alpha}\sigma\sigma\omega$, v.26) and 'gave up' ($\acute{\alpha}\phi\acute{\iota}\eta\mu\iota$, v.27)? Certainly they indicate wilfulness, a theme which is strongly reinforced by the context. Those who do such things 'know God's decree', but deliberately choose to violate it (v.32). Further, 'exchanged' in verse 26 recalls the use of the same verb in the previous verse: 'they exchanged the truth about God for a lie'. And this in turn harks back to v.23: 'they exchanged (ἀλλάσσω) the glory of the immortal God for images'. So the choices of verse 26 are manifestations of a more fundamental choice. What the persons concerned have 'exchanged' or 'given up' is God and his order for human relationships, in favour of their own alternative pattern of relating. It is homosexual behaviour in general which is condemned, not merely conversion to it by people who were formerly heterosexuals.

And finally, 'consumed with passion' (v.27). This expression emphasises the completeness with which those who engage in the acts described are in the grip of their own desires. And they are so because they have been 'given up' to those desires by God. The desires themselves are 'dishonourable' and the acts to which they give rise are 'shameless'. The verb 'consumed' (ἐκκαίομαι), with its connotations of self-immolation, anticipates the explicit reference to self-inflicted judgment which follows (v. 27b). Further, in view of the wider framework of thought, it is not possible to limit the reference to only one category of homosexual activity: acts which are lustful and irresponsible rather then committed and loving. In terms of Paul's own thought the passions and acts he speaks of are dishonourable, not because they are unloving but because they are unnatural. They represent sexual desire indulged outside the framework of the created order. Again, it is homosexuality in general which is condemned here, just as it is idolatry in general which is condemned in verses 20-25.

With these particulars in mind we are now ready to widen our focus again. How do these references to homosexuality relate to the broader framework of Paul's thought?

It should be noted, first of all, that homosexuality as such is relatively incidental to the argument as a whole. The principal sin here, the root from which all else flows, is idolatry, the refusal to acknowledge God as creator and to give him the honour which is his due (vv. 18-25). The movement is from idolatry, to sexual immorality in general (v. 24), to homosexuality (vv. 26-27), and then to other moral offences (vv. 28-31). So Paul does see a close connection between idolatry and sexual licence in particular; other kinds of moral evil are a less direct consequence of it. In this his thought is closely aligned with the Wisdom of Solomon, especially 14:12: 'The invention of idols is the root of immorality'. But it would be unnecessarily restrictive to limit his reference simply to the immorality practised in the name of religion in the various pagan cults. Like the author of Wisdom, Paul sees idolatry as a source of moral corruption that blights the whole of human life. Sexual immorality is mentioned first as the link between the cultic and non-cultic spheres, not to limit its reference to the former. The fact remains, however, that homosexuality is one of a long list of evils here, and there is no suggestion that it is worse than the others.

The more fundamental affinity, however, is with the Law, and specifically with Leviticus 18 and 20. There, as we have seen, homosexuality, like adultery and incest, is part of what it means to be 'like the nations'. Here it is part of what it means to be pagan, an idolater. And in both places, if our analysis has been correct, the theological basis of what is being said lies in the foundational creation material of Genesis 1 and 2. Although the rhetorical purpose is different, the basic stance towards homosexuality is the same. Fundamentally, the biblical view about the legitimacy or otherwise of homosexual behaviour does not change from the Old Testament to the New.

There is a recognition in verse 26 that homosexual acts arise from an underlying condition: 'dishonourable passions'. But in the overall logic of the passage this condition arises from rejection of God. There are larger issues here. There are already hints, in the reference to creation, that Paul has the long view in mind: the fall of the entire human race in Adam, not just the rejection of God by individuals. He will spell this out explicitly in 5:12-14. And if this is so there must be a sense in which the state of mind which gives rise to the acts is inherited. There is a sense in which the individual is predisposed to such acts by birth into a race that has already rejected God. But such predisposition, in Paul's mind, does not excuse the acts themselves. Each individual must choose between the lusts of their heart and God's decree which prohibits their indulgence (v.32). Furthermore, if there are specific 'passions' that give rise to homosexual acts, there are also 'lusts' that give rise to sexual immorality in general (v.24), and 'a base mind' which gives rise to murder, slander and the other evils listed in verses 28-31. In other words, in Paul's thought, a predisposition towards homosexual behaviour does not make it any more excusable than a predisposition to adultery or murder.

Finally, all of this must be set in the context of Paul's rhetorical purpose. His aim is not to single out one particular group as worse sinners than others, but to establish that all alike are guilty. He sees humanity as consisting of two groups: Jews and Gentiles (2:9-10; 3:9) and he does not underestimate the differences between them. The Jews have the law and the Gentiles don't. But his point is that at the most fundamental level they are both the same. He begins with a generalisation ('all ungodliness and wickedness of men', 1:18) and ends the same way ('all men, both Jews and Greeks, are under the power of sin ... all have sinned', 3:9, 23). In chapter one the focus is on the Gentile world, in which idolatry is the cardinal sin. But then in chapter two he turns his attention to the Jewish world, where the cardinal sin is self-righteousness. Paul's argument in Romans 2 is that the Jews, who have the law, have not in fact kept it, and are therefore just as guilty as the Gentiles they condemn. Indeed, they are more so because of the greater privileges they have had (2:24; 3:1). It is his hard and impenitent heart that condemns the Jew (2:5). His condemnation of others is a cover for his refusal to face up to his own sinfulness.

Paul, of course, was well qualified to speak on this subject because of his own impeccable past record in Judaism (Gal 1:13-14). Like Jesus, he saw sins of the spirit (especially pride and hypocrisy) as just as damning, or more so, than sins of the flesh. If he is hard on practising homosexuals in chapter 1, he is even harder on those who self-righteously condemn them in chapter two. But his ultimate purpose is not to induce hopelessness or self-loathing in either. Quite the contrary. In the longer perspective of Romans his purpose is to establish the guilt of all only in order to show the relevance of the gospel for all (3:23). His argument revolves around two principles: God's wrath (his just judgment on sin) and his righteousness (his activity of putting people right with him). The latter is put into effect objectively by the saving sacrifice of Christ, and subjectively by a response of faith. Paul insists that we acknowledge sin as sin, our own as well as others'. We have all sinned; that is the judgment we must accept if we are to know the joy of forgiveness. So paradoxically, the denunciation of homosexual behaviour in 1:26-27 is part of a general indictment which opens out into a message of hope. And the hope perspective which is developed doctrinally here is sustained in the more directly pastoral material of the letters which follow Romans in the canon.

Although it has been denied, there can be little doubt that Paul refers specifically to homosexual behaviour in his list of vices 1 Cor 6:9-10.

> Do not be deceived; Neither the sexually immoral (πόρναι) nor idolaters nor adulterers nor male prostitutes (μαλακοί) nor homosexual offenders (ἀρσενοκοῖται) nor thieves nor the greedy nor drunkards nor slanderers nor swindlers will inherit the kingdom of God (NIV)[12]

Of the two relevant terms, μαλακοί and ἀρσενοκοῖται, the latter is particularly transparent, reflecting closely the LXX of Lev 20:13 (cf. 18:22): 'Whoever lies with a male [μετὰ ἄρσενος κοίτην] as with a woman, they have both committed an abomination'. The order, too, is the same as in Leviticus: first heterosexual offences (adultery) then homosexual behaviour (Lev 18:19, 22; 20:10, 13). The other term, μαλακοί raises more complex questions. Its literal meaning is 'soft', and in the LXX and the NT (apart from here) it is used only of things - a soft tongue (Prov 25:15), soft words (Prov 26:22), soft garments (Matt 11:8; Luke 7:25). But in classical authors of the first century BC to the third century AD it is also used as technical term for boy prostitutes.[13] Philo is particularly harsh on

---

[12] The RSV disguises the reference to homosexuality by rendering μαλακοί and ἀρσενοκοῖται by the single term, 'sexual perverts'.

[13] BAG cites Diogenes of Halicarassus (I BC), Dio Chrysostom (I-II AD), Vettius Valens (II AD) and Diogenes Laertes (III AD).

youths who dress themselves as women for such purposes, and describes such degeneracy as μαλακία.¹⁴ It could be, therefore, that Paul has this particular practice in mind in his use of the term here. But there are a number of considerations against this. The first is the fact that it is linked here with ἀρσενοκοῖται, for which no such technical usage is attested.¹⁵ The second is the general nature of the other vices in the list: idolatry, adultery, drunkenness and so on. Each indicates a broad area of misconduct rather than something narrow and specific. And finally, there is the connection with Leviticus, with its proscription of homosexuality in general. Apart from the specific connection with the Mosaic law via ἀρσενοκοῖται, there is the broader connection via the Judaism in which Paul was raised.

In view of all this it seems best to follow C. K. Barrett¹⁶ in taking μαλακοί and ἀρσενοκοῖται as complementary terms, intended to cover the full range of homosexual behaviour. μαλακοί, via its classical usage, has connotations of passivity; receptivity to homosexual advance. ἀρσενοκοῖται, via Leviticus, has more active connotations ('lie with a man as with a woman'). They therefore lend themselves very well to the kind of complementary use which I am suggesting. If this is so, Paul takes the same basic stance towards homosexuality here as in Romans 1. There is also a similar association of homosexuality with idolatry, and with sexual immorality in general (v.15; cf. Rom 1:24-27). But the form and direction of his argument is quite different.

In Romans 1-3 Paul was working with the fixed categories of Jew and Gentile. Here in 1 Corinthians 6 he is operating with the fluid categories of the unrighteous and the saints (v.1). As the opening verse of the chapter makes clear, 'the unrighteous' is not fundamentally a moral term, but a technical term for unbelievers (v.6), those who still belong to

---

[14] *De specialibus legibus* 3.37-39. Cited by G. D. Fee in *The First Epistle to the Corinthians* (NICOT; Grand Rapids: Eerdmans, 1987), 243 n.22.
[15] Fee, 244.
[16] *A Commentary on the First Eistle to the Corinthians* (Black's New Testament Commentaries; London: Adam and Charles Black, 2nd ed., 1971), 140.

the old, fallen order of things, which Paul calls 'the world' (v.2). The moral evils of verses 9-10 are characteristic of the unrighteous, but they are symptoms of their condition rather than the essence of it. What ultimately defines the unrighteous is their unbelief, their solidarity with the world rather than the kingdom of God. In contrast to them are 'the saints', those who have been washed, sanctified and justified in the name of Christ and in the Spirit of God (vv. 1, 11). 'Saints' is not fundamentally a moral term either, but a technical term for believers, people who have been transferred into the new order of things by the gracious work of God for them and in them rather than by their own moral effort. The good news is that it's possible to pass from one category to the other: 'such were some of you, but you were washed ...'. The warning is that, in the last analysis, a person's standing in Christ is inseparable from behaviour. The Corinthians must take care not to be deceived (v. 9); those who behave like the unrighteous will not inherent the kingdom of God. Saints must behave like saints, and it is their behaviour, in the long term, that will reveal those who are truly saints and those who are not. In Romans Paul was concerned to show that Jew and Gentile are fundamentally the same, and how all alike need to be justified by faith in Christ. Here he is concerned to show that the saints and the unrighteous are fundamentally different, and to challenge the Corinthians to exhibit that difference in their behaviour.

With that broad picture in mind, there are several things to be said about the significance of the reference to homosexuality in this passage.

First, it occurs within a framework of eschatology. Romans 1 moved against the background of the first things, creation and fall. 1 Corinthians 6 moves against the backdrop of the last things, the coming kingdom of God, and this raises the stakes very high. Some will inherit the kingdom of God; others will not. In this context the issue of homosexual behaviour takes on a new urgency. The choice to persist or not to persist in it has eternal consequences.

Second, it is mentioned in close association with 'washing', 'sanctification' and 'justification', 'in the name of the Lord Jesus Christ and the Spirit of our God'. Verse 11 is full of terms which, in one way or another, refer to the process of renewal which has now entered its final phase through the work of Christ and the outpouring of the Spirit. Homosexual activity is mentioned in a context where change is on the agenda, change of a radical kind, effected by God himself.

Third, homosexual behaviour is mentioned as characteristic of 'the unrighteous' (v.9), that is, those who are not yet regenerate. It is an aspect of solidarity with 'the world' (v.2), or in terms of Leviticus 18 and Romans 1, part of what it means to be pagan. At once, however, we must remind ourselves that it is only one of many such characteristics. Greed, drunkenness, and many other things are equally symptomatic of the same condition (vv. 9-10).

Fourth, practising homosexuals, no less than other sinners, are potential candidates for regeneration. 'And such were some of you' (v.11) makes it clear that 'the unrighteous' is not a closed category; exit from it is possible, and the Corinthians themselves are living proof of this. They have been washed, sanctified and justified in the name of Jesus Christ and in the Spirit of our God.

But finally, regeneration necessarily entails forsaking the kinds of behaviour listed in verses 9 and 10, including homosexual behaviour. The whole rhetorical thrust of the passage is aimed at establishing this point, as we have seen.

One last passage remains to be considered before we draw this study to a close, and that is 1 Tim 1:8-10:

> the law is not laid down for the just but for ... immoral persons, sodomites, kidnappers, liars, perjurers, and whatever else is contrary to sound doctrine.

'Sodomites' here translates the same term, ἀρσενοκοῖται, that we have just met in 1 Corinthians 6, and the same strong connection with the law is evident both from the word itself and from the context in which it occurs. The reference to 'genealogies' and 'teachers of the law' in verses 4 and 7 make it all but certain that 'the law' which Paul[17] has in mind is the law of Moses.[18] The list of vices in these verses is a catalogue of acts which were understood in rabbinic thought to be either directly or indirectly proscribed by the law.[19] Paul not only recognises that the law prohibits homosexual acts, but endorses this law as 'good' (v.8). In this Paul is in complete agreement with the 'teachers of the law' he has just mentioned.

He does have a serious disagreement with them, however, and this brings us to the heart of what this passage is about. The men Paul is in dispute with do not use the law 'lawfully', that is, in accordance with its true nature and purpose (v. 8). This is explained in verse 9: the law is not laid down for 'the just', but for 'the lawless and disobedient, for the ungodly and sinners, for the unholy and profane'. And it is the term 'sinner' which is picked up in what follows: 'Christ Jesus came into the world to save sinners. And I am the foremost of sinners, but I obtained mercy ...'. 'Sinner' is what Paul was; 'just' is what he has become. We must conclude therefore, that in Paul's thought here, the 'just' person is not so much a morally upright, respectable person as a pardoned sinner. This pardon is made available through the work of Christ (v. 15) and is received by faith in him (v. 16). The message that announces this is 'the glorious gospel of the blessed God' with which Paul has been entrusted (v. 11). In Paul's thought, the law is not in conflict with this gospel. Indeed, the types of behaviour which the law categorises as wrong are contrary to

---

[17] Authorship is of I Timothy is disputed. I accept Pauline authorship, but the argument being advanced does not depend on this. It depends solely on 1 Timothy being canonical.

[18] See also 4:3 (abstinence from foods), and cf. Titus 1:10 (those of the circumcision) and 1:14 (Jewish fables).

[19] J. N. D. Kelly, *A Commentary on the Pastoral Epistles. 1 Timothy, II Timothy, Titus* (Black's New Testament Commenatries; London: Adam & Charles Black, 1963), 12. It begins with six general offences against God (cf. the first table of the Decalogue) followed by a series of offences which violate the first five commandments of the second table: murder of parents (5th commandment), murder in general (6th), fornication and homosexuality (7th commandment, which was held to refer to sexual vice in all its forms), kidnapping (8th commandment, which was held to include 'stealing' persons, see Ex. 21:16), and lying and perjury (9th).

the 'sound doctrine' to which Paul himself is committed. How then do Paul's opponents misuse the law? They do so by directing believers to it as the resource (indeed the only resource) they need for a godly life. In so doing they deflect attention from the gospel of grace with its transforming power. For Paul the law is the handmaid of the gospel. For his opponents the law is everything.

Paul agrees with his opponents, then, that homosexual acts are wrong. The law of Moses stands as an uncompromising witness to this fact. But this is something that Paul affirms almost in passing. The main thrust of what he is saying lies elsewhere. 1 Timothy begins and ends with grace (1:2; 6:21). The aim of Paul's charge is 'love' (1:5), and there is a strong note of 'hope' that runs through the whole letter: 'Christ Jesus our hope' (1:1), 'our hope is set on the living God (4:10), 'eternal life' (1:16; 6:12), 'the life to come' (4:8), 'the appearing of our Lord Jesus Christ (6:14-16), and 'the future ... life that is life indeed' (6:19). It is worth pausing to mark carefully this strong note of eschatological hope, since it is so often overlooked in discussion of the Pastoral Epistles. The gospel is a message of hope for sinners, and Paul knew that if it had so transformed his own life, there was no sinner beyond its reach. The bedrock on which it rests is the faithful saying of 1:15, 'Christ Jesus came into the world to save sinners', and the goal towards which it points is 'the appearing of our Lord Jesus Christ' when hope will be consummated in the 'the life to come' (6:14; 4:8).

It is on this note of hope that the Bible makes its last reference to homosexuality.

The book of Revelation: the final triumph of God's purposes

At the end of the Bible, as at its beginning, there is no explicit reference to homosexuality. There is a strong affirmation, however, of God's sovereignty as creator. The last three chapters of Revelation are replete with many references to the opening three chapters of Genesis: the final destruction of 'that ancient serpent, who is the Devil and Satan', the tree of life, the river of life, the abolition of death and the lifting of the curse. The message is plain, God's original purposes will be achieved. The created order will not only be maintained, but perfected, and every challenge to it finally put down. The key to this outcome is Jesus Christ, who is both redeemer and judge. The dominant note is one of celebration, but it is judgment as well as salvation that is celebrated, for both alike express the truth that God reigns. The question for his creatures is whether or not they will acknowledge this fact. The chilling list of 'outsiders' in 21:8 and 22:15 is a sad reminder that some will defy God to the end and reap the terrible, and eternal consequences of their choice. But even here the Bible maintains its balance. Settled opposition to God can be evidenced as much by faithlessness and lying as by sexual misconduct, and even this is referred to only by general term πόρνος ('sexually immoral person'). The final warnings of Scripture apply as much to heterosexual sinners as to homosexual ones.

Final reflections on Genesis 1-3

The consistent position of Scripture is that homosexual acts are morally wrong because they are contrary to the revealed will of God. His will is revealed explicitly in the law of Moses, and the sexual ethics enshrined there are unequivocally endorsed by Jesus and the apostles. But whenever this explicit command of God is referred to, there is nearly always an underlying allusion to creation. That is, the law simply makes explicit what is implicit in creation itself. What the biblical writers do not do, however, is unpack this basic theological datum. They do not reflect on *how* the biblical accounts of creation embody the will of God for human sexuality. It may be legitimate and even necessary for us to do this, but we must recognise that we are engaging in a form of argument which is our own, and not that of the Bible itself, and therefore any conclusions we come to must be tentative. With this caveat in mind I offer the following theological reflections.

What is it to be human?

The fundamental relationship in Genesis 1 is the relationship between God and man (humankind), not the relationship between man and woman. To be human is to be made in the image of God, and in terms of the data which Genesis 1 provides, this means to be a creature addressed by God and therefore responsible to God. The male-female polarity is introduced to enable humankind to fulfil the mandate to fill the earth and subdue it, but it is not the essence of what it is to be human. That's why our identity as human beings can never be found in our sexuality, and why sex can never be redemptive. Our identity lies in our relationship with God, and redemption consists of restoring that relationship. It also explains the strangely 'sexless' view of heaven which we find in the NT. The end of redemption is not sexual fulfilment but something that transcends it.

What is it to be man and woman?

The division of humanity into man and woman has important consequences for our self-awareness and potential for development as human beings. We derive our identity as human beings ultimately from God. Nevertheless a man knows himself to be man only in relation to woman, and a woman knows herself to be woman only in relation to man. Man cannot fully develop his proper identity and potential as man unless he recognises his complementary dependence on woman, and woman cannot develop her proper identity and potential as woman unless she recognises her complementary dependence on man. Man cannot be fully man by relating only to men, and woman cannot be fully woman by relating only to women. Complementarity and mutual need must be fully accepted if we are to be men and women as God intended us to be. The 'one flesh' union between a man and woman in marriage is the most intimate and perfect expression of our 'man-ness' and 'woman-ness' that is possible. To make any other form of sexual expression ultimate is to deny our true identity as men and women.

Can the procreative and unitive functions of human sexuality be separated?

Much depends on this. If the two functions can be separated, or if sex itself can be separated from either or both of them, then all kinds of activities become legitimate. Reflection must surely begin with the fact that we have two complementary creation accounts in Genesis and that human sexuality is only part of the total picture that they present. They deliver their message about human sexuality in exactly the same way that they deliver their message about God (transcendent and immanent) and man (made in the image of God, made from the dust). The complementary ideas that they present are separable conceptually, but not practically. They are two aspects of the one indivisible reality. The same is true of our sexuality. Its procreative and unitive functions can be separated conceptually, but they cannot be divorced in practice without doing violence to the God-given character of human sexuality itself.

It should be remembered, however, that Genesis 1-2 is much more about relationships than sex as such. The main requirement is that sex takes place within a relationship in which both the procreative and unitive aspects of human sexuality are accepted as God-given and the responsibilities that they bring are accepted. Homosexual behaviour divorces sex from procreation; casual sex of whatever kind divorces it from its unitive function.

Which is primary: the procreative or unitive function?

This is a difficult issue to resolve, mainly because the primary biblical data is ambiguous. One could argue that procreation is primary because this is what is highlighted in the first account of creation. Gen 1:1–2:3 sets the basic framework for the discussion of human sexuality; the unitive aspect of sex, a second order issue, is then explored in 2:4-25. On the other hand, one could argue that the account of the 'one flesh' union of the man and the woman is the climax of the total presentation of God's creative activity which spans Genesis 1 and 2 as a whole, and therefore the unitive aspect of sex is primary.

Dogmatism is entirely out of order here, but there are several considerations which make the second option the more likely one in my judgment. The marriage of 2:18-25 is the high point of human well being as willed and brought about by God, from which the Fall of chapter 3 then takes place. Further, the procreative aspect of sex is something that human beings have in common with the animals. This is self-evident of course, but particular attention is drawn to it in Genesis 1 by the double occurrence of 'Be fruitful and multiply' in verses 22 and 28 (with reference to animals and human beings respectively). In contrast to this, the one flesh union of man and woman in Genesis 2 is presented as something conferred by God on the human pair alone, and something which sets them apart from the animals. And finally, it is the unitive aspect of human sexuality which receives special emphasis in the teaching of Jesus. Note, for example, Matt 19:4-5, where 'he ... made them male and female' (Gen 1:27) is followed immediately by 'For this reason a man shall leave his father and mother' (Gen 2:25). That is, the primary purpose of the male-female distinction is the one flesh relationship of marriage.[20] Procreation is normally possible only in the first half of such a relationship, but the relationship itself is intended to be life-long, and the unitive function of the relationship, rightly understood, is not in the least diminished by the loss of procreative capacity.[21]

---

[20] Allowance must be made for the fact that the context is a discussion about divorce. But this does not empty the quotations from Genesis of relevance to our topic. Jesus answers the divorce question by referring to the essential character of marriage. It is entirely probable that one of the possible grounds for divorce that Jesus' questioners had in mind was barrenness, the absence or loss of procreative capacity. But given the fact that marriage is essentially unitive, the only ground for dissolution that Jesus will allow is adultery.

[21] The starting point for discussion of the vexed question of contraception must be a consideration of the context in which the original command to procreate was given, namely, an empty world needing to be filled and subdued. Given the primacy of the unitive function of sex, and the changed circumstances in which we now find ourselves, responsible use of contraception to regulate procreation is fully justified in my judgment.

We may reasonably conclude, then, that the unitive function is primary. But it does not follow from this, however, that homosexual marriage is a legitimate option, because the 'one flesh' unity of Genesis 2 is predicated upon the male-female difference between the partners, and even in the post-Fall situation, no other kind of marriage is ever countenanced by Scripture.

Is homosexuality natural?

In biblical terms, the difference between 'natural' and 'unnatural' has to be understood in terms of the effects of the Fall on the created order. The Fall does not render everything unnatural. Much that happens after it, including the proliferation of the human race and the emergence of arts and crafts, is entirely in keeping with what was anticipated in creation itself. Such things are 'natural'. But the Fall introduces another category of things which stem from human rebellion against God and are contrary to his will for human life as expressed in the created order. These are 'unnatural'. The law of Moses specifies many of them and indicates clearly that they are to be rejected as unacceptable patterns of behaviour. The contexts in which homosexuality appears in Scripture places it firmly in this category. It is an expression of our fallenness rather than our createdness. This rules out in principle any talk of a homosexual condition as 'the way God made me'. It may be part of the way I am, even part of the way I was born, but it is not how God intends me to be. It is something to be resisted with God's help.

Isn't love the ultimate moral criterion?

In Genesis 1 God's word orders the physical realm. He speaks and gives the world its shape, separating waters from waters, sea from land and light from darkness. In chapter 2 he speaks again and orders the moral realm. He tells Adam what he may and may not do. He separates right from wrong. It's within this context of God's authoritative and powerful speaking that human sexuality comes into existence and finds its proper character and role. Its goodness (and the text is very insistent that it *is* good) arises from the blessing and command of God which brings it into existence and orders it according to his will. It is not love which is ultimate, but the word of God. And this same principle is maintained throughout the Bible. Love is never divorced from obedience.

> In emphasising love for God and neighbour as the two great commandments, Jesus and his apostles did not discard all other commandments. On the contrary, Jesus said 'if you love me you will keep my commandments', and Paul wrote, 'Love is the fulfilling (not abrogating) of the law'. Love needs law to guide it. ... Love is concerned with the highest welfare of the beloved. And our highest human welfare is found in obedience to God's law and purpose, not in revolt against them.[22]

Creation, Redemption, and Community

The creation accounts point strongly to the fact that God wills us to live in community rather than isolation. The procreative aspect of sex leads naturally to all the complex human relationships which comprise human community and belongingness: parents and children, brothers and sisters, friends and comrades. The man who is 'alone' is in a condition that is 'not good' (Gn 2:18), and one of great need. This need is recognised by God and met by the provision of a wife, and ultimately of family, clan, people and nation. Human beings cannot realise the good that God intends for them alone. Wholeness is possible only in community, of which marriage is the basic institution.

Of course we live in a world that is sadly changed from that of Genesis 1-2. For many people marriage is not possible, and a strong homosexual tendency, whatever its cause, is undoubtedly a significant factor in some cases. The love which God commands us to have both for him and our neighbour demands that we recognise the needs of such people and actively seek their good. And this can finally be achieved only by them being loved and incorporated into

---

[22] J. R. W. Stott, *Issues Facing Christians Today* (Marshalls, 1984), 315.

Christ and his people. Where homosexual behaviour is involved, repentance will be required, as it is for all sinners, but love precedes repentance rather than being a condition for it: 'God shows his love for us in that while we were yet sinners, Christ died for us'. The final outcome of the redemptive process which God puts into effect after the Fall is a community of loving obedience in which all may find acceptance by grace. The truth is that we are all sinners, and our true identity is not 'homosexuals' or 'heterosexuals', but human beings, made in the image of God, fallen, but still loved by God, and (if we will have it so) his sons and daughters through Christ.

Exploring further

1. How are the Old Testament laws against homosexual practices relevant for a Christian approach to homosexuality today?
2. In what particular ways is the life and teaching of Jesus the key to a truly Christian response to sexuality?
3. On reflection, do you feel that your own past attitude to homosexuals and homosexuality has been fully biblical? What changes, if any, do you hope to make in the light of this paper?
4. How can Christians have meaningful dialogue about homosexuality with people who do not share their belief in the Bible's inspiration and authority?
5. How can Christian congregations be accepting of homosexual persons without condoning homosexual activity?

MEDICAL AND PSYCHOLOGICAL PERSPECTIVES ON HOMOSEXUALITY

Philip Mitchell
Associate Professor, School of Psychiatry,
University of New South Wales

Synopsis

There has been a recent intense upsurge of scientific and media interest in reports of possible biological explanations for homosexuality. This article reviews these studies, focusing particularly on investigations of prenatal hormonal exposure, brain structure and genetic factors. The implications for both the theologian and pastor of such approaches to explaining homosexuality are discussed.

A married Christian man undergoing treatment for depression recently confided to me his sexual attraction to males. Although he had never acted upon this attraction, it had been present for many years, despite his conscious attempts to suppress and control it. He wrote to me:

> ... the more I'm honest with myself, the more certain I am that I am at the least bisexual and that I've always known it at some level. I wonder how much of my heterosexuality is really learned behaviour.

Why had this Christian man experienced homosexual inclinations for much of his life, despite a conscious dislike of such desires? It did not seem reasonable to posit a conscious decision to become homosexual in this case, as he regarded such impulses as sinful, though no more so than other behaviours:

> At least I'm free of the issue of a hierarchy of sin. All sin is repugnant and abhorrent by definition ...Should I ever act on it (and I am conscious of the fact that there but for the grace of God go I) it would be a form of adultery...

So how do we make sense of his homosexual inclination? Was it the result of distorted early life experiences, perhaps in his relations with his parents? Or was it the outcome of biological processes, perhaps an aberrant gene (or genes), or some subtle abnormality in the hormones to which he was exposed during development as a fetus in his mother's womb?

Whilst there are no clear answers to these profound questions, there has been a recent plethora of scientific and media interest in such issues. On March 15, 1993, the 'Washington Post' published an article entitled 'Study of twins suggests lesbianism has a genetic component'. The correspondent began:

> Is homosexuality, at least in part, the product of biological causes? ... The findings bolster the tentative but increasingly plausible theory that human sexual orientation - heterosexual as well as homosexual - is influenced to a significant degree by biology and is not exclusively a matter of upbringing or 'lifestyle choice'.

In a similar fashion, under the headline 'Born Gay?', an article in *Time* magazine July 26, 1993 commented:

> The origins of homosexuality may never be fully understood and the phenomenon is so complex and varied - as is every other kind of love - that no single neat explanation is likely to suffice to explain any one man or woman, let alone multitudes. But the search for understanding advanced considerably last week with the release of new studies that make the most compelling case yet that homosexual orientation is at least partly genetic.

Such claims and debate in both the scientific and wider community compel us to examine the evidence upon which claims about the origins of homosexuality are being made, with their obvious potential political and theological ramifications. In this article I will overview the significant recent scientific evidence and discuss its relevance to an informed theological and pastoral response to homosexuality.

Prior to examining possible causative factors, however, it is necessary to review current writings on the definition and prevalence of homosexuality. An awareness of such issues is necessary as these impact upon the methodology of studies examining the origins of homosexuality.

How is homosexuality defined and rated?

'Gender identity' is generally defined (Stein et al, 1993) as an inner sense of being male or female. 'Sexual orientation' refers to the individual's erotic response tendency as reflected in dreams or fantasies orientated to the same or opposite gender. The sexual orientation, however, may be discrepant from that suggested by the gender of the person's actual sexual partner. That is, overt sexual behaviour may differ from sexual orientation.

There have been two differing approaches to the definition of homosexuality. The majority of researchers have employed overt social sexual behaviour to define homosexuality or heterosexuality as categorically distinct behaviours. The alternate approach, espoused by Kinsey (1948, 1953) and more recently McConaghy (1993), has been to view sexual orientation as a continuum. Using this approach, individuals may be rated as either exclusively homosexual or heterosexual, or as having some ratio of heterosexual to homosexual orientation (e.g. 90% heterosexual and 10% homosexual).

Kinsey devised the Kinsey heterosexual/homosexual scales (Kinsey, 1948, 1953) which included four items related to sexuality, i.e. self-identification, attraction, fantasy and behaviour. Each item was rated on a 7-point scale, with 0 representing exclusive heterosexuality, 6 exclusive homosexuality, and 3 representing equal degrees of each.

What is the prevalence of homosexuality in the community?

The Kinsey studies

The 'classic' studies of the prevalence of homosexuality were those undertaken by Kinsey in 1948 and 1953. These were studies of volunteers.

In the 1948 report on males, Kinsey found that 4% were exclusively homosexual, 50% exclusively heterosexual and 46% were somewhere in between. Furthermore, he stated that

50% of white males had experienced erotic responses to males, whilst 37% had at least one experience of homosexual arousal to orgasm. Thirteen percent had more homosexual than heterosexual experience.

The 1953 study of females found lower rates of homosexual orientation and behaviour than that demonstrated in males. Twenty-eight percent of the women surveyed had experienced erotic responses to females. Twenty percent had had specific homosexual contact, whilst 14% of the total had experienced homosexual arousal to orgasm.

Two comments about the Kinsey data are necessary. First, surveys of volunteers are prone to distortion due to the biased reports of those coming forward for such research. Second, a significant proportion of homosexual behaviour occurs only during adolescence, a period during which self-concepts are evolving. Unlike Kinsey, many other authorities exclude such adolescent behaviour, considering it to be of only transient significance (though recently McConaghy (1993) has argued strongly against this).

Recent prevalence studies

Since the reports of Kinsey there have been a number of subsequent surveys of rates of sexual behaviour in the community. Two recent studies are worthy of particular note as they were both random surveys of very large population samples. It should be noted that both surveys examined actual sexual practice, rather than sexual orientation.

Johnson et al (1992) reported a random-sample survey of 18,876 British males and females aged between 18 and 59. Examining male lifetime homosexual behaviour, they come up with the following findings: 6.1% had some homosexual experience; 3.6% had at least one homosexual partner in their lifetime; 1.4% had at least one homosexual partner in the previous five years; and 1.1% had at least one homosexual partner in the previous year. Unfortunately, rates of homosexuality in the female sample were not included in this report.

A French group (the A.S.C.F. Investigators) reported similar findings in their survey published in the same issue of the scientific journal 'Nature' (ASCF Investigators, 1992). They undertook a random telephone survey of 20,055 male and females between 18 and 65 (with only 24% refusing to participate). First, with regard to males, they found 4.1% with at least one occurrence of homosexual intercourse during their lifetime, 1.4% in the previous 5 years, and 1.1% in the previous year. Second, the corresponding female rates were 2.5% over a lifetime, 0.4% in the previous five years, and 0.3% in the previous year. Interestingly, in line with Kinsey's concept of a continuum of sexual behaviour, they found that 82% of males who had had homosexual intercourse had also had heterosexual intercourse, while for females the corresponding rate was 78%.

These methodologically superior studies indicate lower rates of homosexual activity than those reported in the much-publicised Kinsey surveys. They indicate a lifetime experience of homosexual intercourse occurring in 4-6% of the male population - a much lower figure than Kinsey's 37%.

Is homosexuality a psychiatric disorder?

Until 1973, homosexuality was officially considered to be a form of mental illness in the highly influential American Psychiatric Association (APA) diagnostic nomenclature, as represented by the DSM (Diagnostic and Statistical Manual). Whereas homosexuality was listed in DSM-I (1952), it was excluded from DSM-II (1968), though 'ego-dystonic homosexuality' (where the person is concerned about his/her homosexuality) continued to be listed until DSM-III-R (1987).

Why was homosexuality dropped as a psychiatric disorder? This was largely a political process. In 1973 a Task Force of the APA argued that homosexuality did not meet the criteria for a mental disorder, that is, it did not regularly cause subjective distress and was not usually associated with some generalised impairment in social effectiveness. The report was put into effect after being passed by both the annual general meeting of APA and a referendum of the entire membership.

Did that vote imply either an endorsement of homosexuality as a variant of normal sexual behaviour, or that it was of equal value to heterosexuality? No. It was argued in a tabled position paper at the time that it would be no more appropriate to label homosexuality a mental illness than other socially unacceptable behaviours such as racism or fanaticism. Although these behaviours may not be considered optimal, they are nonetheless not indicative of mental illness.

THEORIES ABOUT THE CAUSATION OF HOMOSEXUALITY

There have been a number of theories on the origins of homosexuality which have derived from differing theoretical schools. While traditional explanations were derived from psychoanalytic and behavioural approaches, more recent theories have derived from the biological sciences. Such a shift is not peculiar to studies of homosexuality, but is merely reflective of the burgeoning of knowledge in the neurosciences and the consequent application of such knowledge to explaining human behaviour. It is likely that both approaches will provide useful contributions to this ongoing debate.

Psychosocial Theories

Psychoanalytic theories

Freud believed that heterosexuality was the natural outcome of development and described a variety of origins for homosexuality. Later analysts such as Bieber viewed homosexuality as invariably a sign of psychopathology. Bieber (1962) believed that the genesis of male homosexuality lay in the mother establishing a closely binding, often explicitly seductive relationship with her son, leading to sexual overstimulation. This, said Bieber, produces intense guilt and anxiety about future heterosexual behaviour. Bieber described the fathers as detached, hostile and rejecting. He saw the father as not acting as an adequate male model to protect his son from demasculinisation. Bene (1965) placed more emphasis upon the father-son interaction, believing that the pressure of a poor relationship with the father was more common than undue attachments to the mother.

Learning theory

McGuire articulated the behavioural approach in 1965. He stated that an initial deviant homosexual experience in childhood or youth supplies the basis for subsequent fantasies which accompany masturbation. Regular subsequent contact with males then leads to arousal in both fantasy and eventually, reality.

Biological Theories

Prenatal hormonal exposure

Evidence from animals exposed to opposite-sex hormones and hormonal abnormalities in humans has been used to argue for the prenatal hormonal hypothesis, namely, that homosexuality is due to abnormalities of hormone exposure during fetal development. Specifically, it has been argued that homosexual males (like heterosexual females) are exposed during fetal development to low levels of male sex hormones (androgens), while homosexual females are exposed to high levels of these hormones (like heterosexual males).

Before examining the relevant studies, an introduction to normal sexual development is necessary. In the developing fetus, females possess two X sex chromosomes (XX), whereas males possess one X and one Y sex chromosome (XY). In the absence of the Y chromosome the ovaries, uterus and fallopian tubes develop internally, and female external genitalia develop. Similarly, without a Y chromosome, a female brain development occurs. The differences between male and female brain structure are subtle and poorly understood. There is some evidence, however, mainly from animals, of sexual dimorphism (or differences) in the structure of some brain areas, perhaps related to sexual behaviour or functioning.

In the presence of a Y chromosome testicular growth occurs. The testes produce two hormones of developmental importance. Muellerian inhibitory hormone (MIH) suppresses the development of the fallopian tubes and ovary, allowing the internal male structures (the vas deferens and prostate) to develop. Testosterone leads to the development of the masculine external genitalia, and also determines male brain development.

Animal studies

In animals, masculinisation of the brain is responsible for the reflex masculine response of 'mounting' to sexual stimulation. The analogous female response is 'lordosis' - receptive pelvic presentation to the male. A number of studies (well reviewed by Byne and Parson, 1993) have demonstrated that male rats castrated just after birth (thereby reducing their testosterone production) demonstrated lordosis, whereas female rats exposed to androgens during early development demonstrated mounting behaviour. Such animal models have been used as analogies for human homosexual behaviour. Some, however, (e.g. Byne and Parson, 1993) have argued that there are significant limitations to the extrapolation from these animal studies to human homosexuality. For example, human sexual behaviour is motivated and not reflex in character, and the activity is between two homosexual partners.

Human studies

Clinical hormonal disorders provide useful 'experiments of nature' to test the effect of hormonal abnormalities on sexual orientation and behaviour.

a. *Syndrome of testicular feminisation:*

   In this disorder patients are genetically male (XY), have testes (and therefore produce androgens), but have a reduced number of androgen receptors (proteins on the surfaces of cells that androgens 'lock into' to produce their effects). Because of the lack of these receptors, the cells are 'blind' to the androgens, and act as if there are low levels of those (as in normal females). These males therefore develop female genitalia and are reared as girls. Their abnormality is recognised at puberty when they fail to menstruate. In puberty they develop an interest in males. While some have used this as an analogy to argue for a hormonal origin to homosexuality, this argument ignores the fact that these patients developed a *female gender identity* due to their sex of rearing.

b. *Syndrome of congenital virilising adrenal hyperplasia:*

This disorder occurs in genetic females (XX). The adrenal glands (near the kidney) which normally produce small amounts of androgens in females are overactive, leading to androgen levels akin to those found in males, with some consequent masculinisation of the external genitalia. Usually this abnormality is detected at birth and the genitalia are surgically corrected. The overactive adrenals are suppressed and they are reared as girls. Whilst there is some increase in 'tomboyism' there is no clear increase in homosexual orientation, indicating that lesbianism is unlikely to be the result of prenatal androgen exposure.

c. *Hormonally-treated pregnancies:*

Synthetic progestogens (sex hormones) have been used medically to prevent miscarriages in some women during pregnancy. Various progestogens have either androgenic or antiandrogenic properties, suggesting the potential for significant effects upon the prenatal androgen exposure of both male and female fetuses. Although there have been a number of studies of sexual orientation of males and females exposed to such hormones during fetal development, there is no consistent evidence for an effect on later sexual orientation (Reinisch et al, 1991).

Abnormalities of brain structure

In animals several areas in the hypothalamus (a part of the brain responsible, amongst other functions, for regulation of hormone production and menstrual cycles) are of different sizes in males and females. It has been suggested that this sexual dimorphism (distinct structural forms in males and females) may relate to both hormonal and behavioural differences between the sexes. Such sexual dimorphism has not been so clearly demonstrated in humans, though there has been interest in the role of the INAH (interstitial nuclei of the anterior hypothalamus) - the human equivalent of one of the sexually dimorphic areas of the rat hypothalamus.

While there have been a number of studies examining abnormalities of brain structure in homosexuality, probably the most significant has been that of Le Vay (1991). Le Vay reported a post mortem brain study of an area of the INAH (INAH3) in homosexual males, heterosexual males and heterosexual females. The INAH3 region is usually larger in males than females. Le Vay found INAH3 to be the same size in homosexual males as it was in heterosexual females (and correspondingly smaller than that found in heterosexual males). He concluded that the INAH3 region may be responsible for sexual orientation.

Although this is an important finding it needs to be replicated by other research groups before it can be accepted as established fact. This is particularly so as there were some methodological limitations to the study. Whereas all the homosexual males died of AIDS, only a fraction of the comparison group died of this disease. Additionally, the determination of sexual orientation in the comparison group was made on inadequate sexual histories, so there is some room for doubt that all the comparison group were definitely heterosexual.

Genetic studies

As indicated in the opening discussion of this article, the main focus of both the media and scientific community in recent months has been upon reports of potential genetic causes of homosexuality.

Prior to embarking upon an examination of these reports, an overview of the general principles of genetic studies is necessary. How does one demonstrate the genetic origins of a condition or behaviour, particularly one as complex as sexual orientation? The first step is the demonstration of increased rates of the disorder in the families of identified individuals, though this procedure cannot discriminate between a genetic origin and environmental factors (such as the role models of parents, shared culture, and so on). The second step is the demonstration that the condition is shared more frequently (has a 'higher concordance') between identical (monozygotic - one egg) than non-identical (dizygotic - two egg) twins. This is because monozygotic twins share all of their genes, whereas dizygotic twins share no more genes than normal siblings. The third, and most definitive step is 'linkage analysis', whereby the disorder is demonstrated to be 'linked' to a specific gene or chromosomal region.

a. Twin studies

The earliest genetic study of homosexuality was that of the well-known psychiatric geneticist Kallmann (1952), who reported 100% concordance for homosexuality in monozygotic twins, compared to only 12% in dizygotic twins. Whilst superficially this provided extremely strong support for the hypothesis of a genetic causation of homosexuality, there were problems with the study, particularly as all the twins were drawn from psychiatric or correctional institutions. Furthermore, no subsequent studies have found concordance rates remotely approaching 100%. Unfortunately, there was no further significant interest in this matter until recent years because of the pre-eminence of psychosocial approaches in the intervening years.

Within the last few years, however, there have been a number of important twin studies which have generated intense interest. There have been four major reports. Two of these have arisen from Bailey and Pillard in the United States. In 1991 they reported significantly higher concordance rates for male homosexuality in monozygotic twins (52% concordance) compared to dizygotic twins (22%). Two years later (Bailey et al, 1993) reported similarly significantly higher rates of female homosexuality in monozygotic (48%) compared to dizygotic (16%) twins. A similar finding from Australia (Buhrich et al, 1991) reported higher rates in monozygotic twins in a combined study of male and female homosexuals.

King and McDonald (1991) however, found no difference between identical (10%) and non-identical (8%) twins in a British population.

Can these twin studies be regarded as definitive in confirming a genetic basis to homosexuality? Whilst authorities such as Bailey and others would argue in the affirmative, other workers are more cautious. Baron (1993), in particular, has argued strongly that the methodological limitations of the published studies necessitate leaving this question open. He highlights several issues: i) all studies have used a categorical, not dimensional definition of homosexuality (i.e. all subjects were categorised as either homosexual or not. There was no reported ratio of homosexual to heterosexual feelings); ii) subjects were ascertained through advertisements in gay and lesbian journals, leading to potential biases in those twins entering the studies; and iii) the assignment of twins to dizygotic or monozygotic status was not precise (DNA methods were not used).

An additional concern is that two of the three positive studies arose from the same research group, while the Australian study was undertaken in collaboration with the same authors. Replication studies by independent researchers are clearly necessary.

b. Linkage study

Perhaps the most important study of the genetics of homosexuality published hitherto is the recent linkage study of Hamer et al (1993), from the National Institutes of Health in the U.S. There were two stages to this report. First, the researchers found higher rates of homosexuality (7.5%) in the maternal uncles and cousins of homosexuals than would be expected in the general population, whereas the rates in paternal uncles and cousins were no higher than normal. This finding suggested to the researchers that a gene for homosexuality may reside on the X-chromosome (inherited from the mother).

They then examined for potential linkage between a number of regions on the X-chromosome and homosexuality in 40 pairs of homosexual brothers. They found a strongly significant sharing of one of the normal variants in the DNA of a particular region of the X-chromosome, much higher than would be expected by chance. This, the authors contested, indicated that a gene for homosexuality could be in this area.

What do we make of this recent study? Whilst methodologically impressive, experience in recent years with other similar linkage reports in behavioural disturbances would suggest caution. For example, a dramatic report that alcoholism was associated with a variant of the dopamine receptor has not held up in subsequent studies. Neither have reports of genes for schizophrenia or manic-depressive illness, despite much scientific and media interest when they were published. This finding of linkage of homosexuality to a region on the X-chromosome should therefore be regarded as only tentative until it is either confirmed or refuted in future reports. At present this is not definite knowledge.

In the meantime, what if a gene or genes for homosexuality were to be confirmed at some future date? How would we conceptualise this? Linkage or twin studies only indicate if a gene is, or is not, involved. These techniques do not tell us whether the genetic differences indicate a disease or an unusual variant of normality. That is, they do not distinguish between whether homosexuality is a disorder, or whether it is a variant of sexual behaviour analogous to blue or green eyes both being normal variants of eye colour. That differentiation is in the realm of the theologian or philosopher - science can go no further than demonstrate associations.

The confirmation of a gene would also have potential political ramifications. The *Time* magazine article referred to above quoted Eric Juengst of the U.S. National Centre for Human Genome Research: 'This is a two-edged sword. It can be used to benefit gays by allowing them to make the case that the trait for which they're being discriminated against is no worse than skin colour. On the other hand, it could get interpreted to mean that different is pathological'.

Concluding reflections, and implications for theologians and pastors

At present there is no convincing demonstration of a definite psychological or biological cause of homosexuality. Despite that, there is a growing body of literature, particularly in the field of genetics, which suggests that it is not beyond the realms of possibility that a causative process, for at least some of those with homosexuality, may one day become established fact. However, the current literature would suggest that a single process accounting for all is unlikely and that a multifactorial understanding is most appropriate.

What do these studies contribute to the Church's theological understanding of homosexuality? Some in the gay community are obviously arguing that the demonstration of physical cause will obviate all responsibility for a homosexual orientation and preclude the interpretation that it is voluntary 'sinful behaviour'.

Whilst the issues are obviously complex, I would have a few responses. First, it may well be that for at least some individuals the roots of their homosexuality (be those in genetics or early life experiences) are beyond, or minimally within their control. God, who is a fair and compassionate arbiter, is the only one who can determine this. Second, the demonstration of a physical cause in some does not necessarily make this an acceptable variant of normal behaviour. It may very well be interpreted that this is indicative of homosexuality being a pathological aberration from normal sexual functioning.

What is the implication for the pastor? Irrespective of the final outcome of the current scientific questioning, the example of Christ compels us to blend an appropriate yearning for right behaviour with more than a touch of His compassion.

REFERENCES

A.C.S.F. Investigators, *AIDS and sexual behaviour in France.* Nature 360:407-409, 1992.

American Psychiatric Association, *Diagnostic and Statistical Manual of Mental Disorders.* Washington, DC, American Psychiatric Association, 1952.

American Psychiatric Association, *Diagnostic and Statistical Manual of Mental Disorders,* 2nd Edition. Washington DC, American Psychiatric Association, 1968.

American Psychiatric Association, *Diagnostic and Statistical Manual of Mental Disorders,* 3rd Edition, Revised. Washington, DC, American Psychiatric Association, 1987.

Bailey, J.M., & Benishay, D.S., 'Familial aggregation of female sexual orientation', *Am J Psychiatry* 150:272-277, 1993.

Bailey, J.M., Pillard, R.C., Neale, M.C., Agyei, Y., 'Heritable factors influence sexual orientation in woman', *Arch Gen Psychiatry* 50:217-223, 1993.

Bailey, J.M., & Pillard R.C., 'A genetic study of male sexual orientation', *Arch Gen Psychiatry* 48:1089-1096, 1991.

Baron, M., 'Genetics and human sexual orientation', *Biol Psychiatry* 33:759-761, 1993.

Bene, E., 'On the genesis of male homosexuality: An attempt at clarifying the role of the parent', *British Journal of Psychiatry* 111:803-813, 1965.

Bieber, I., *Homosexuality: A psychoanalytic study*. New York, Basic Books. 1962.

Buhrich, N.J., Bailey, J.M., & Martin. N.G., 'Sexual orientation, sexual identity, and sex-dimorphic behaviours in male twins', *Behav Genet* 21:75-96. 1991.

Byne, W., Parsons, B., 'Human sexual orientation: The biological theories reappraised', *Arch Gen Psychiatry* 50: 228-239, 1993.

Dorner, G., *Hormones and brain differentiation*. New York, Oxford, 1976.

Hamer, D.H., Hu, S., Magnuson, V.L., Hu, N., Pattatucci, A.M.L., 'A linkage between DNA markers on the X chromosome and male sexual orientation' *Science* 261:321-327, 1993.

Johnson, A.M., Wadsworth, J., Wellings, K., Bradshaw, S., Field, J., 'Sexual lifestyles and HIV risk' *Nature* 360:410-412, 1992.

Kallman, F.J. 'Comparative twin study on the genetic aspects of male homosexuality', *J. Nerv Ment Dis* 115:282-298, 1952.

King, M., McDonald, E., 'Homosexuals who are twins: A study of 46 probands', *British Journal of Psychiatry* 160:407-409, 1992.

Kinsey, A.C., Pomeroy, W.B., & Martin, C.E., *Sexual behaviour in the human male*. Philadelphia, PA, WB Saunders, 1948.

Kinsey, A.C., Pomeroy, W.B., & Martin, C.E., *Sexual behaviour in the human female*. Philadelphia, PA, WB Saunders, 1953.

Le Vay, S., 'A difference in hypothalamic structure between heterosexual and homosexual men'. *Science* 253:1034-1037, 1991.

McConaghy, N., 'Homosexuality/heterosexuality - Sissiness and tomboyism', *In Sexual Behaviour: Problems and Management*. Plenum Press, New York, 1993.

McGuire, Carlisle and Young, 1965.

McWhirter, D.P., 'Biological theories of sexual orientation', *In Review of Psychiatry* Vol. 12, American Psychiatry Press, Washington DC, 1993.

Reinisch, J.M., Ziemba-Davis, M., Sanders, S.A., 'Hormonal contributions to sexually dimorphic behavioural development in humans', *Psychoneuroendocrinology* 16:213-279, 1991.

Stein, T.S., 'Overview of new developments in understanding homosexuality', *In Review of Psychiatry* Vol. 12, American Psychiatric Press, Washington, DC, 1993.

Exploring further

1. How should the Church respond if a gene for homosexuality is confirmed?
2. Is homosexuality no more aberrant than a difference in skin or eye colour?
3. How should the Church balance biblical teaching with scientific evidence in a controversial area such as homosexuality?
4. How would you understand it if your son or daughter was homosexual? How would you respond?

HOMOSEXUALITY AND ETHICS

Michael Hill
Lecturer in Ethics, Moore College

Synopsis

Two elements generate a moral dilemma for bible-believing Christians. The first element is that the Bible consistently condemns homosexual behaviour. The second has to do with mounting evidence that some people are predisposed towards sexual activities with members of the same sex because of genetic and/or psychological factors. Strong forces push these people in one direction while the traditional Christian ideal moves them in another. Is it fair to put these people through the trauma of such conflict and tension?

One suggestion has been made that for people in this situation the biblical ideal might be re-written to take account of the forces in their lives. The moral requirement placed on the absolute invert might be reduced to that of fidelity only. This article examines the suggestion and rejects it for a number of reasons. An alternative is proposed. Using the distinction between justifying and excusing, a change in the application of the moral ideal is mooted.

Locating the issue

Barry Webb has convincingly argued that the Scriptures consistently condemn homosexual acts as morally wrong.[1] His examination of the relevant scriptural passages makes it clear that homosexual behaviour is against the revealed will of God. Moreover, it is against the general will of God. That is, it is not a particular prohibition given for a particular reason at a particular point for a particular group in salvation history. Rather the condemnation has to do with God's universal and abiding purposes encapsulated in the accounts both of creation and redemption.

---

[1] See Barry Webb's article in this volume.

After a review of recent medical and psychological studies, Philip Mitchell concludes that while there is 'no convincing demonstration of a definite psychological or biological cause of homosexuality' 'it is not beyond the realms of possibility that a causative process...may one day become established fact'.[2] As a result 'it may well be that at least for some individuals the roots of their homosexuality (be those in genetics or early life experiences) are beyond, or minimally within their control'.[3]

The possibility that some homosexuals are subject to forces over which they have little or no control generates a moral problem. Can these people be held morally responsible for their actions? If not, what is to be done at the moral level? Will it be necessary to re-write moral ideals in regard to sexuality for these people? Will it not be morally unfair to demand of these people the same behaviour we demand of the general population? Is it not immoral to burden these people with moral baggage impossible to carry?

In response to these questions some theologians have suggested what has been called the 'Compromise' position.[4] The position presents a different ideal for those in this unique category. This paper attempts an analysis and critique of the Compromise position and the questions and issues that give rise to it.

A matter of definition

Webb noted that the Scriptures focused on homosexual acts and not on disposition. They condemned overt homosexual behaviour. This is a legitimate focus given our topic but it does not encompass the whole of our topic. The word 'homosexuality' can refer to an *orientation* or an *action* or *class of action*. Just as the Scriptures would lead us to use the term

---

[2] See the previous article, 118.
[3] Ibid.
[4] See, for example, the articles by H. Kimball Jones and Charles E. Curran in *Homosexuality and Ethics*, (ed) Edward Batchelor (Jr), (New York, Pilgrim Press, 1980).

to refer to an act or class of actions, others use the term to refer to a disposition or orientation. Dwyer's definition is helpful at this point. He defines homosexuality as a *'preference, on the part of adults, for sexual behaviour* with members of their own sex'.[5] This definition will allow that someone may have a homosexual orientation and not engage in homosexual acts nor be willing to engage in homosexual acts. It will also allow that someone in prison might engage in homosexual acts and prefer heterosexual relationships outside of prison. Such persons would not be homosexual because their preference is not for sexual behaviour with the same sex. According to this definition sexual conduct during adolescence should not be counted as truly homosexual since that is the period when people come to a mature or settled disposition in relation to their sexuality. We are not so much concerned with the process of reaching a settled disposition but with the disposition itself and its maturity. The term 'sexual behaviour' refers to those actions or infatuations which lead to physical fulfilment or orgasm.

Our definition will prevent misleading claims. Earlier this year on one of the morning television shows in Sydney it was claimed that thirty-seven percent of the male population was homosexual. An advocate of the homophile movement based this claim on the evidence adduced in the Kinsey Report. Kinsey had observed that thirty-seven percent of males have at least one experience of homosexual arousal to orgasm. Using Kinsey's evidence to draw such a conclusion ignores the fact that people might go through various experiments or thoughts in their psycho-sexual development without being habituated to them.

Two further terms must intrude at this point. These are the terms 'inversion' and 'perversion'. 'Inversion' refers to an exclusive and involuntary sexual orientation towards others of the same sex, 'perversion' indicates sexual attraction or involvement with members of the same sex by a person who is

---

[5] J.C. Dwyer, *Human Sexuality: A Christian View*, (Kansas city, Sheed and Ward, 1987), 64. The emphasis is his.

naturally heterosexual in orientation.[6] It is the apparent exclusive and involuntary nature of the inverts disposition which has given rise to the Compromise argument.

The compromise argument

Kimball Jones has developed an approach which recognises that homosexual activity is against the will of God but does not involve homosexuals in an impossible struggle.[7] He concedes that homosexual acts are contrary to the will of God for human sexuality but argues that our moral judgments must give more importance to the reality of sin within the objective order of this world. Absolute inverts, it is suggested, have a fixed and unchangeable nature. Celibacy and sublimation are not possible. This fixed nature is the result of the effects of sin. Since the absolute invert cannot change his or her nature and is not responsible for being what he or she is, then the only moral requirement placed on them can be that they act responsibly within their given framework. Responsibility, in this case, would mean that they be loving and other-person centred and act in the same type of way that heterosexuals are required to act in their heterosexual relationships. A permanent relationship would be required.

Charles Curran, a Catholic theologian, also affirms that for the absolute invert 'a somewhat permanent homosexual union is the best, and sometimes the only, way for him to achieve some humanity'.[8] But Curran objects to Jones' use of the doctrine of sin. For Curran the structure of human sexuality remains even though the invert cannot live according to it because of the 'infecting power of sin'.

Jones' position is best understood if we make a distinction between the objective and subjective orders of

---

[6] See the glossary of terms at the beginning of Andrew Shead's paper in this volume.

[7] H. Kimball Jones, 'Toward a Christian Understanding of the Homosexual', *Homosexuality and Ethics*, ed. Edward Batchelor, Jr, (New York, Pilgrim Press, 1980), 105-113.

[8] C. E. Curran, 'Homosexuality and Moral theology: Methodological and Substantive Considerations', *Homosexuality and Ethics*, 94.

reality. Jones argues that because of sin the objective order of particular people's sexual nature (the absolute invert) is changed from that of the creation order. Not only is it changed but it is fixed. The only moral domain of responsibility for the invert is the subjective one.

On the other hand Curran declares that '(s)in affects this present order but does not do away with all the moral distinctions which are based on both creation and redemption'.[9] Man must try to overcome sin even in the objective order. Every attempt should be made to overcome the homosexual condition but where these efforts fail Curran argues that some form of permanent homosexual union may be the best moral option.

A fixed and unchangeable nature

Two basic premises underpin the Compromise Argument. It is asserted that (i) absolute inverts have a fixed and unchangeable nature, and that (ii) celibacy and sublimation are not possible. Neither of these premises have been secured by recent research. While the first of these premises has considerable support, evidence for the second has been severely prejudiced or limited by the attitude and approach of the homophile movement who have concluded that homosexual activity is morally proper and that there is no need for celibacy or sublimation. Indeed, the suggestion of either of these courses of action meets with hostility because it is seen to have moral implications which are unacceptable.

But let us suppose that the first premise was established as fact. What consequences would it have for the Compromise argument? It certainly would not establish the second premise. Indeed, the claim that inverts have a fixed and unchangeable nature is ambiguous. Is the reference to their biological or psychological nature?

Let us suppose that some biological factors were involved. How ought this evidence to be interpreted? Given that humans are far more complicated than rats, and that human

---

[9]   Ibid.

behaviour is motivational and not reflex in the area of sexuality, the most reasonable response would be that it is not directly determinative or causal. It would be best to see the biological elements as providing boundary conditions for sexual behaviour.

The notion of boundary conditions can be explained and illustrated by drawing an analogy with a pin-ball machine. A pin-ball machine consists of an enclosed arena containing upright columns or pins. A ball is released into the arena at a certain velocity and in a set direction. The force and direction of the ball plus the location of the pins and the shape of the arena (especially any slope on the floor) will determine where the ball comes to rest. The more pins there are into which the ball might collide the more difficult it is to control the result. The shape of the arena and the position of the pins can be arranged in various ways. To change the arrangement is to change the boundary conditions in relation to the activity of the ball. In a similar way biological factors such as brain structure and genetic inheritance form the boundary conditions for sexual behaviour.

The analogy can be pressed a little further. A player has control over the force with which a ball is released into the pin-ball machine. The player controls this by governing the tension of the spring which powers the ball. The similarity here is only partial and occurs at one particular point. Just as the player has control over the release of the ball so the conscious subject (the ego) has *some* control over sexual drives. The extent of the control will vary in accordance with a number of factors. One of these will be hormonal. Others will be the strength of will and the commitments of the subject in question. Outcomes can and will vary according to the different boundary conditions and the varying motivational forces. Boundary conditions set a field and limit the possibilities but they are not totally determinative.

Despite the truth of all of the above the evidence appears to be that there may be some people whose biology and psychological history generate within them sexual forces of great magnitude set in a specific direction. The intensity and dimensions of these sexual feelings make them appear overwhelming and irresistible. Given the present state of knowledge and research in this area it will be difficult to determine whether the overwhelming nature of the desires are due to biological factors which cannot be changed or psychological factors which might be altered.

All of this begs the question of whether or not change is morally required. This is a question that we must face in due course but for the moment it is enough to note that a reasonable theoretical understanding of the biological and psychological factors does not preclude either celibacy or sublimation. Both may be difficult but they are not impossible. One factor that makes both these options look unacceptable in our generation is an acceptance of the ethic of self-fulfilment and self-satisfaction. In many parts of our community there is not just a passive acceptance of the ethic but a violent commitment to it. This violent commitment has been fuelled by the doctrine of individualism propagated since the time of John Locke.

No neutral starting-points

An issue that comes out of our discussion of the aetiology of homosexuality is one that has often been ignored. Its moral significance is undeniable. This is the issue of starting-points.

Within Christian circles where moral rules or principles have been treated as absolute it has frequently been assumed that everyone starts equi-distant from the moral ideal. If we take the exhortation not to steal it has been imagined that the moral effort not to steal is the same for everyone. Yet this is obviously not the case. A rich person in Australia or America who has abundant resources to meet the need of their family is under far less moral pressure than a poor person in a third world country who sees their children starving while next door is a wealthy land-baron who has accumulated wealth at the expense of those around him.

Even if we concede the tentative nature of the conclusions in relations to the causes of the homosexual condition, the direction in which the evidence moves us is significant. Whatever the orientation the moral pressure generated by sexual desires will vary according to hormonal and psychological factors. Orientation also will be influenced by biological and psychological elements. There will be a great variety of starting points and some people will have to move a lot further to reach the ideal than others. Surely this is a factor of moral significance.

A Christian view of human sexuality

Before we can examine the suggestion that the sexual ideal ought to be modified for those with certain starting-points it will be necessary to delineate the nature of the ideal and the reasons for its adoption. It may be that certain modifications cannot be made without destroying the ideal itself.

The method of determining a Christian ethic will be as important as the content of the ethic itself. The justification of an ethic has much to do with its acceptance. It is never enough just to declare one's ethic. With this in mind I shall not only outline the content of a Christian view of sexuality but the method by which it was arrived at and by which it is secured.

As evangelical Christians we are committed to the authority of the Bible for matters of faith. The building of what might be called a Christian or biblical ethic requires a number of stages. Commencing with the texts of Scripture an overall picture of salvation history is built up.[10] Moral values and judgments are understood in the particular context of salvation history in which they are found. On the basis of this overall picture of salvation history the enterprise of biblical theology is undertaken. The presuppositions and implications of the particular phases of salvation history are teased out in their own terms. Finally, all these clues and fragments are put together in a systematic way.[11] Again, this

---

[10] Salvation history refers to the time-frame of God's activity in history to bring about salvation.

[11] In his paper Barry Webb has gone through the first few stages. He has exegeted passages in their historical context and then gone on to try to understand their meaning for us given their place in the programme of salvation history. I shall concentrate on the systematic stage. This is

is done in such a way as not to damage the logic or fabric of the biblical material. In this way a systematic theology is achieved which can then be taken and applied to the contemporary situation. This whole procedure for understanding the Bible and its message for today has to be a fellowship activity if it is going to be faithful to the Bible itself. Individual engages with individual in the community of faith and that understanding which integrates the most clues in the best way gains an authority and acceptance.

The Bible does not present us with an extensive discussion of human sexuality. But it does give us control beliefs and other clues which provide boundaries or a framework through which and by which we can experience and understand our sexuality.

Fundamental to that framework and understanding is the schematic outline of the shape of reality given in Genesis 1-3. Both Jesus and Paul refer back to this passage when faced with questions on sexuality and marriage. There is no doubt about its authority within Scripture. The normative pattern projected here is that a man cleaves to his wife and the two become one flesh (Gen 2:24). The Hebrew word for cleave accentuates the unity of the one flesh. It is used of incurable diseases which cannot be separated off. As the biblical revelation unfolds it is clear that this pattern is not one option among many. Adultery, fornication, homosexuality, bestiality are all condemned.

It is clear that the marriage pattern, and therefore sexual behaviour, is to fit the general pattern of mutual love relationships propagated in the Scriptures (see Eph 5:21-23). The sex drive and its associated emotions and aesthetical evaluations are all to be shaped by love. That is, libido and eros are to be shaped by agape. And the purpose of all this is not self-satisfaction or even mutual satisfaction but unity or oneness. This unity or oneness is not just a biological oneness but a oneness that is of the whole person. In

---

the stage where the universal truths are located. Because these elements are universal and apply to everyone in every context they can be applied to our present situation.

Ephesians 5:32 the one flesh imagery is seen as analogous to the relationship between Christ and the church.

The unity envisaged in the Scriptures is not just a unity of purpose; it is far more profound. For the word 'unity' we may substitute 'completeness'. The man and the woman find their perfection in each other because their natures are complementary. The unity envisaged is found when two complementary beings, the man and the woman, come together and give themselves in service to one another at every level. Sexual union becomes a symbol of this holistic union. Each partner gives themselves to the other as a person through the body. The goal of human sexuality is completeness and unity and it only comes with the binding together in love of two complementary beings—the male and the female.

The nature of this complementarity is complex. Many simplistic and sexist accounts of complementarity have caused this concept to be spurned and rejected. It is not the complementarity of opposites whereby the male is active and the woman passive or the male is rational and the woman is emotional and so on. Briefly, it is the complementarity of overlap and emphasis.[12]

The centrality of love

Jesus' reaction to both the keepers of the law and the keepers of the traditions in Jewish society highlighted and secured the primacy of love in Christian ethics.[13] Other NT writers take up and maintain this tradition. In this context love is a thing of the heart. In today's context this would mean that it was an emotion. But the biblical concept of heart goes back to an OT concept where the heart was the cluster at the core of a person's being. It included thinking, feeling, evaluating,

---

[12] There is no space to develop this idea but for a stimulating discussion of the biological basis for gender differences see Robert D. Culver, 'Does Recent Scientific Research Overturn the Claims of Radical Feminism and Support the Biblical Norms of Human Sexuality?', *JETS* 30/1 (March 1987), 39-47.

[13] See Matthew 22:34-46; Mark 12:28-34; Luke 10:25-28.

willing, and choosing. It is that cluster at the centre of a person's being that issues in intentions and then actions.

Love is an aspect of personal relationships. It can be directed towards our heavenly Father or towards our neighbour. 'Love' is a value term and love involves honouring a thing in accordance with its nature. If we honour God according to his nature as a loving and providing Creator then we will trust and obey him. If we love our neighbour made in the image of God then we will be committed to the good of that neighbour.

Love, the good and creation

Love of neighbour necessitates a commitment to the good of the neighbour. Oliver O'Donovan has shown that there is a logical and necessary relationship between created order and the good.[14] The argument demands the use of the distinction between generic and telic order. A simple illustration should assist our understanding.

Suppose a manufacturer makes a knife for use at the dinner table. Its purpose is to cut food. The manufacturer chooses the metal for the knife carefully. The criterion used is the metal's ability to sustain a sharp edge. Like most household knives it has a handle, a flat blade, and a blunt end. If the metal used in the manufacture is high-tensile steel it may not only sustain a sharp edge but it may be able to be used for a lever to open jars and even a screw-driver to tighten up some loose screws on occasions.

Suppose someone from a primitive culture visited the manufacturer's kitchen and came upon the knife. Knives were not part of the visitor's culture and he was bemused by this instrument. After a lengthy stay in the house he discovers that the instrument can be used for cutting, screwing, and levering. Does this mean that the instrument was not a knife but a multi-purpose instrument? Not at all. It fails as a lever because it is not long enough to give an advantage in many

---

[14] See Oliver O'Donovan, *Resurrection and Moral Order*, (Leicester: Inter-Varsity Press, 1986), Chapter 2.

situations. It also snaps under what may be considered moderate pressure for most levers. It fails as a screw-driver because the handle is the wrong shape and will not facilitate turning in the hand. The blunt front edge will not sit properly in the slot of many screws.

The nature and/or use of the supposed 'knife' could be interpreted in several ways. These ways correlate with some philosophical and theological attempts to interpret 'creation' in the history of western thought. One possibility is that the visitor could view the manufactured item as a unique particular. It was a something—a know-not-what—which could be used for several purposes. In this case the thing itself would not have a purpose but the user could use it to serve the purposes that he had. Because the thing has no specific end or purpose—no telos—it could not be identified as a *kind*. It could be used as a kind of thing but it would not be a kind.[15] The reason for this is that kinds are identified by their ends or purposes.

On this view the thing would not be formed or manufactured with a purpose in view. Its properties would be accidental and unintentional. A purposive mind would seize upon its properties and give it a purpose or multiple purposes. It could become a loose sort of kind in that it might be recognised by its uses and become a three-in-one screwdriver cum knife cum lever with limited and weak uses as a screwdriver and lever.

Another approach, which is logically linked with the nominalist approach, is one which recognises kinds but declares that it is the human mind which gives kinds their purpose by discovering a use. It is the human will which chooses to use things in certain ways which determines the kind of thing they are even though the properties which allow it to serve in this way are objectively in the thing itself. Because of its focus on choice and will this approach has been known as voluntarism. Both nominalism and

---

[15] Historically speaking, this is the approach of nominalists who refuse to recognize kinds and only recognize particulars.

voluntarism 'assign purposiveness exclusively to the human will'.[16]

The doctrine of creation presented in Scripture will not allow either nominalism or voluntarism. Some kinds exist out there in the world and they have ends or purposes. These kinds we call natural kinds.[17]

Male and female created he them

The point of the previous discussion is that there are different sexes and that God has ordered them according to their kinds to their own ends. These ends constitute God's purpose. In the realm of gender, which includes the sexual, the end or purpose of the male is unity with the female; a unity which requires complementarity.

We have seen that love involves a commitment to the good of others. We have also seen that the good is dictated by the telos and that the telos is intrinsically tied to the nature or form of a thing. So the sexual good of a male or female can only come about when libido and eros are shaped by agape and directed towards a member of the opposite sex. The good of both is achieved through the completeness that comes from the complementarity of each sex.

It follows that if a male loved another male he would want to secure what was good for that other male. According to the Bible that good is found in completeness that comes from a complementary relationship. Hence if love seeks the objective good of the other it would want a male-female relationship for the other.

It will be helpful here to draw a distinction between the objective good of the person which depends upon his or her nature and its telos and pleasing the other which depends upon the subjective desires of the person. If love requires a commitment to the good of the other then it may be claimed

---

[16] O'Donovan, *Op Cit*, 46.
[17] For example, in Genesis 1 mankind is given fruit and green plants for food. We need to note that natural kinds are not the only kinds found in creation.

that homosexuals do not love one another in the biblical sense even when they do that which pleases the other.

The result of a permanent homosexual union would be mutual satisfaction but not completeness for this requires complementarity. Now while completeness encourages permanency, satisfaction does not. Satisfaction may be found elsewhere, in another person. The evidence that homosexuals are far more promiscuous than heterosexuals tends to support this conclusion.[18]

Permanent homosexual unions would be different to the ideal of union presented in the Scriptures and it is questionable whether these unions would be permanent and exclusive. The matter of permanency and exclusivity is a question open to empirical examination or research. If both partners were other-person centred then such relationships might be permanent. But it would not be biblical for the relationship would have to operate on the basis of subjective desires rather than objective nature or need.

Sin, structures and responsibility

The earlier distinction we made between objective and subjective good in relation to Kimball Jones' argument now becomes clear. The objective good is based on the form or nature of the person. The form or nature is that given to it by God. But, like the nature of our knife, many forms are ambiguous. Human nature, especially the sexual aspect of human nature, can be put to other ends or purposes. Moreover, as we have seen, it is possible that the very structure of a person can be changed so that it makes other ends or purposes more likely or subjectively preferable. The Scriptures themselves recognised such structural changes. Romans 8 speaks about the creation being subject to futility and decay. It anticipates the creation finally being set free from this bondage.

---

[18] A programme on SBS in 1992 revealled the results of research in an English city. It was shown that while heterosexuals were promiscuous, homosexual males had ten times the number of partners that heterosexual males had.

Despite the changes and decay due to sin it is still true to say that our human sexual nature is ordered towards heterosexual relationships. The recognition of this fact led Charles Curran to object to Kimball Jones' position. Curran wanted to maintain that though sin affects this present order it does not do away with all the moral distinctions which are based on both creation and redemption. The reasons for his insistence should now be clear. Much of this paper has been taken up with the effects of sin on human nature not only because I have wanted to endorse Curran's objection but explain my reasons for doing so.

Despite his objection to Jones' position Curran comes to a compromise when he asserts that for the absolute invert 'a somewhat permanent homosexual union is the best, and sometimes the only, way for him to achieve some humanity'.[19] My objections to this compromise are multiple. The first has to do with the distinction previously drawn between being committed to the objective good of the person (a good based on the nature given to persons by God) and a commitment to pleasing the person by serving their subjective desires. Since God is the transcendent Creator He is the One who desired to give human beings the universal nature they have. In honouring people according to their nature we not only secure their objective good, whether they desire it or recognise it, but we please and serve our Heavenly Father by fulfilling His purposes.

It appears that Curran has forgotten the thrust of Jesus' reflection on the Torah. Not only are we to love our neighbour but we are to love God. We love God by honouring his purposes. A Christian locked into a fixed homosexual nature must resist his nature—a structure affected by sin—because his desire is to please God. Our vertical relationship with God and our horizontal relationships with our neighbours are linked together. Unlike the humanist we cannot imagine that we are just dealing with natural structures. We are also dealing with the One who ordered these structures according to his purposes.

---

[19] *Op Cit*, 94.

My second reason for rejecting Curran's position is that it is not the loving thing to do in terms of the Scriptures. It is not loving since it is not committed to securing the good according to God's purpose or in accordance with nature. A somewhat permanent union may be the lesser of two evils but since God cannot condone evil it is not an option.[20]

Thirdly, I have my severe doubts that a somewhat permanent union is possible amongst all but a very few homosexuals. My doubts do not stem from the seriousness of the commitment that homosexuals might make to one another. Rather it stems from the nature of the homosexual condition and their ability to be monogamous. I have already referred to the study reported on the SBS in 1992 relating to promiscuity amongst homosexuals. The extent of promiscuity amongst homosexual males is confirmed by the Rev. Gary Walker, a pastor at the predominantly homosexual Metropolitan Community Church in Sydney, who indicates that gay men tend to reverse heterosexual courtship procedures. Rather than get to know one another first, they tend to have sex even before exchanging names.[21] From listening to homosexual men explain this behaviour it seems to be driven by a pathological need to be accepted by other men. Whether other men represent a 'father-figure' I do not know but both the drive and the promiscuity are well attested.

Finally, I object to Curran's second order ideal for absolute inverts because we do not seem to adopt this approach to other similar cases. If a person's biological inheritance and social/psychological history predisposes the person to violent behaviour and assault we do not say that it is okay or proper for them to be violent. Rather we restrain them and we try to find means both moral and appropriate to train them not to be violent.

---

[20] This is not to say that I do not have a retrieval ethic. Like the Scriptures (eg on the topic of divorce) I have an ethic which tries to secure the best consequences after some evil, that is, something against the order of nature, has been done. But the Scriptures never recommend evil so that good may abound.

[21] *Good Weekend*, in the Sydney Morning Herald, July 24, 1993. 32.

Someone might object to the analogy above. They might argue that violence is obviously morally wrong while homosexuality is not. But this is to beg the question. It is to limit the notion of harm to what is empirical and natural. Such an argument precludes the supernatural or transcendent level. One cannot do this and faithfully maintain a Christian ethic.

A way forward

Appropriately, the discussion of people biologically predisposed to violence can lead us into a way forward. The way may not be all that everyone wants in this world but that is the nature of the world we live in. Scripture reminds us that we await the consummation of our hope in Christ.[22] We will only have all that we want and need when Christ returns in glory.

Perhaps I can change the example above. Instead of referring to people prone to violence we will refer to those prone to anger. Then many more people will have personal experience that relates to the issue.

If I may be allowed a personal anecdote. Growing up as a twin had a number of advantages. Some of these advantages have only been seen in retrospect but they remain advantages none-the-less. My twin brother was always much less aggressive than I was. He seemed to have been born that way. In the early days he did not seem to have the same adrenalin flow as I did. I was always in more fights and arguments than he was. In fact, he rarely seemed to get into fights or arguments, and, when he did, frequently I would end up in one also trying to protect him in my own paternalistic way.

Becoming a Christian and restraining or controlling my anger and channelling it into positive things was much more difficult for me than it was for my brother. Or, at least I have always reckoned it to be so. Whether it was true that I struggled harder than my brother in this matter or not it is a fact readily accepted and frequently observed that some people, because of their starting-point, expend far more moral energy

---

[22] Romans 8:18ff.

coming up to the ideal than do others. This is an important observation and it has its moral implications. But before we examine these moral implications we need to introduce a distinction which is consequential to them.

In his superb book on abortion, Robert N. Wennberg makes a distinction between excusing and justifying.[23] It is a moral distinction. Justifying, or providing a justification, is what we do when we declare that an act is precisely the one that ought to have been done. On the other hand, when we provide an excuse we acknowledge that an act is not the sort of thing one ought to do but that extenuating circumstances relieve the agent of some or all of the blame.

I want to suggest that this distinction is a legitimate and useful one, especially in relation to the moral dilemma faced by many homosexuals. Homosexuals with a biological inheritance and psycho-social background which predisposes them to partners of the same sex have to expend far more moral energy to maintain the moral ideal than many other homosexuals and heterosexuals. The expenditure of moral energy must be taken into account when moral assessment or evaluation is being made.

We must note that the notion of moral justification can be a misleading one in Christian ethics. Christian ethics really is the task of locating what ought to be done rather than justifying oneself. According to the Christian gospel no one can justify themselves before God. Rather God justifies us in Christ and we then live to please him. Part of the life of pleasing God is taken up with locating what is good and right in His sight. The moral or ethical enterprise is not about establishing one's moral status but pleasing God by doing what is right and good.

Christians who adhere to the gospel can never take the moral high ground and look down on others. Barry Webb has rightly pointed out that we are all sinners. People who expend more moral energy than most of us and still fail to meet the ideal cannot expect that the ideal will be re-written for them.

---

[23] Robert N. Wennberg, *Life in the Balance*, (Grand Rapids, Eerdmans, 1985), 144.

By the same token after making a great moral effort they do not deserve to have the moral ideal dropped on them as though they have made no effort at all or as though they are not morally concerned.

Ethics, pastoral counselling and personal relationships.

The application of the distinction between justification and excusing is not an easy matter. It requires personal judgment and involves a degree of moral responsibility. For this reason people tend to prefer just to lower the moral rule or ideal upon people so that they know they are condemned and feel appropriately guilty.

Again we need to observe that condemnation is only one function of the Christian ethic. The ethic also includes freedom from condemnation and guilt and the desire to please and serve God. Continual sin and failure does not preclude one from the Christian life. Jesus suggested that forgiveness was to be endless.[24]

Whether one is a friend, head of a congregation, or counsellor one will have to make a judgment about whether a particular act was wilful or not. Such judgments require knowledge and the acquisition of this sort of knowledge demands an openness and compassion which draws confession and confidence.

Conclusion

In relation to the homosexual who is disadvantaged by biology and nurture we must acknowledge moral effort. At the same time we still have to recognise that they have failed to meet God's requirement and point them to the way of the cross and forgiveness. We must continue to recognise moral effort where it is expended and reward it with support and understanding. The lack of support and understanding has meant that many Christian homosexuals have abandoned the Christian ideal

---

[24] See Matthew 18:22 and parallels.

and the moral struggle altogether. Like most things the blame for this belongs not just with the individual but with the community as a whole.

BIBLIOGRAPHY

R. T. Barnhouse, *Homosexuality: A Symbolic Confusion*, (New York, The Seabury Press, 1979).

R. T. Barnhouse & U. T. Holmes III (eds), *Male and Female; Christian Approaches to Sexuality*, (New York, The Seabury Press, 1976)

E. Batchelor, *Homosexuality and Ethics*, (New York, The Pilgrim Press, 1980).

P. Coleman, *Gay Christians; A Moral Dilemma*, (London, SCM, 1989).

J. C. Dwyer, *Human Sexuality: A Christian View*, (Kansas City, Sheed and Ward, 1987).

J. P. Hanigan, *Homosexuality; The Test Case for Christian Sexual Ethics*, (New York, Paulist Press, 1988).

O. O'Donovan, *Resurrection and Moral Order; An Outline for Christian Ethics*, (Leicester, Inter-Varsity Press, 1986)

R. J. Magnuson, *Are Gay Rights Right?*, (Portland, Multnomah, 1990).

Exploring further

1. What criteria and procedures can one use to stop the notion of excusing becoming a practice of anything goes?
2. Should a person of fixed homosexual disposition hold a position of leadership in the local congregation?
3. Should we adopt church structures which prevent practicing homosexuals from being active members of local congregations? Would such structures be morally justified?

4. If a local congregation adopted structures which prevented active homosexuals from being members, what ministry could operate at a personal level?

THE RE-ORIENTATION OF HOMOSEXUALS, AND MODELS OF THERAPY

Bill Andersen
Formerly Senior Lecturer in Education,
Sydney University

Synopsis

Granted that it is desirable for anyone with a homosexual orientation to be refocussed sexually the paper examines the feasibility of bringing this about.

A brief survey is made of some of the factors that have been thought to contribute causally to the development of a homosexual disposition, and then an outline is given of a general theory of homosexuality offered by Elizabeth Moberly. Some models of therapy are presented, aimed at reorientation, including the model which flows from Moberly's analysis.

Hope for reorientation lies in the power of God the Holy Spirit, expressed *scientifically* by an ever more adequate theory, *therapeutically* by ever more appropriate forms of procedure, and *personally* by the loving interaction with clients of Christian therapists, mentors and friends, individually and in church groups.

Introduction

Is it desirable for anyone homosexually inclined or anyone homosexually active to be re-focussed or re-oriented? And if this is desirable, is it ever possible?

In the light of the paper, within this series, by Barry Webb, entitled 'Homosexuality in Scripture', it is indeed desirable, for it acknowledges the serious and beneficent purposes of God in creating humans male and female, and the complementarity which is brought to their relationships because they are male and female. Because of God's purposes, heterosexuality is a norm, rather than a preference, established with the best interests of men and women in view.

Granted, then, the desirability of re-orientation in sexual disposition, sexual activity or both, the question of possibility arises. This paper in no way underestimates the difficulties involved in attempting reorientation, nor does it make the facile claim that all those homosexually inclined or active can be re-orientated. All that it affirms is that *some* have been re-orientated, and that this result is made more likely by an understanding of causal factors, the formulation of a satisfying theory, and the development of forms of therapy which take account of both.

Causal factors

The following factors may not, in the long term, be confirmed as *strictly* causal with respect to homosexuality. What can be said is that there appears to be some correlation or plausible connection between the factor concerned and the development of a homosexual orientation, for some of which a combination of factors will be judged causal.

The list is not to be taken as exhaustive, nor can each one be spelled out fully because of the limitations of space. What does seem likely, however, is that for any one person there will be a form of multiple causation, and that for different men and women the particular combination of factors will be different.

1. Biological factors, either hereditary (structural and genetic) and/or congenital (functional and hormonal) are being carefully studied, as was made clear in Philip Mitchell's paper, 'Medical and Psychological Perspectives on Homosexuality'. As that paper affirmed, there are many aspects of biological research which could have a bearing on homosexuality, including the suggestion that there may be a gene which is closely connected. However, in some of these studies it is not clear whether certain abnormalities of brain structure, for example, are a cause or an effect of homosexual activity, while in others, as Mitchell pointed out, a great deal depends on how we

conceptualise what is discovered. A 'special' gene could be regarded as a disease gene, ie as pathological, or as an unusual, but understandable variant of sexual possibility. In any case, every aspect of human personality and action relates to and is influenced by some genetic substratum, but is not for that reason alone thought to be *caused* by that genetic structure in any strong sense.

2. The 'Oedipal' pattern, described by Freud, was one in which there existed a strong sexually-tinged relationship between a doting, demanding mother and her son, exacerbated by a weak father. The corresponding 'Electra' pattern involved a strong relationship between father and daughter, with a weak mother in the offing. Both brought the appropriate Greek myths into modern psychological theory in a way quite startling for the late Victorian audiences upon whom they first fell! For many years the Oedipal pattern was the 'classical' explanation for homosexuality.[1]

While it is true that this pattern has been challenged as the sole causal factor, it is also true that it remains a potent and frequent influence, especially in times of marriage conflict and break-up.

3. A 'blocking' of heterosexual interest can be effected by negative, emotionally-charged instruction from parents or other influential figures; by fear; through negative modelling by parents; by association of heterosexual love with trauma and tragedy; by lack of opportunity; or by social attitudes which denigrate heterosexuality as a norm.

4. The combination of emotional deprivation in early childhood with a normal desire for sexual experience and with initiation, by another, into homosexual acts, even if

---

[1] I have here shorn the original Freudian account of some of its trimmings, such as the assertion that all boys go through an Oedipal stage, and all girls an Electra, and that homosexuality results from the non-resolution of the respective 'complex', prior to the 'latency' period of middle childhood.

these be passive at first, will constitute another causal pattern for homosexual activity.

5. A cultural atmosphere (often termed 'macho') in which masculinity is perceived to be correlated with aggressiveness, ruggedness and muscular development, and in which femininity is connected with intuitiveness, bookishness and artistic interests, makes it likely that rugged males attribute homosexuality or at least 'sissiness' to their more intuitive brethren. Similarly girls who excel in sport or outdoor pursuits may be seen as 'tomboys'. In either case, an external attribution may be matched by an internal 'owning', so that any other causal influences may be exacerbated by this factor.

6. Where there has been some barrier to the receiving of affection from the parent of the same sex, then the man may well seek sexual experience from another man, or the woman from another woman: a form of compensatory activity. This factor has been left to the last to provide continuity with the general theory of homosexuality proposed by Elizabeth R. Moberly.[2]

Moberly's general theory of sexuality

Before attempting an outline of Moberly's theory, a few observations would seem to be needed on the criteria that should be satisfied before a theory is deemed worthy of adoption. From the viewpoint of scholarly Christian commitment, a theory of homosexuality would, at least, need:

1. to do justice to empirical findings;
2. to accord with relevant biblical theology;
3. to display a notable internal coherence among its principles;

---

[2] Moberly's work draws upon psychology and theology, and is expressed briefly in *Homosexuality: a New Christian Ethic*, Clarke: Cambridge 1983. It is based upon eight years' work on research and the development of therapy in the area. Moberly is a member of the Orthodox Church.

4. to manifest greater explanatory power than rival theories; and
5. to suggest fruitful forms of therapy, arising from its contentions.

Further to these very general criteria, it is also highly important, in my view, that a theory should struggle to bring both biological and psychological evidences into interaction with each other, and similarly biological and psychological theorising. To my knowledge, though such attempts have been made in other fields, such as attitude-formation, this has not been prominent, as yet, in the study of homosexuality.

There follows now an outline of the basic principles of Moberly's theory:

1. 'The homosexual condition is itself a deficit in the child's ability to relate to the parent of the same sex which is carried over to members of the same sex in general.'[3]
2. 'Needs for love from, dependency on, and identification with the parent of the same sex are met through the child's attachment to the parent. If, however, the attachment is disrupted, the needs that are normally met through the medium of such an attachment remain unmet.'[4]
3. 'Not merely is there a disruption of attachment, but, further, a...resistance to the restoration of attachment'[5]— a form of repression.
4. This 'repression of the normal need for attachment has to contend...with the drive towards the restoration of attachment...It is precisely this reparative urge that is involved in the homosexual impulse, that is, that this impulse is essentially motivated by the need to make good earlier deficits in the parent-child relationship.'[6]

---

[3] Moberly, 5.
[4] Moberly, 5.
[5] Moberly, 5,6
[6] Moberly, 6.

5. 'The persisting need for love from the same sex stems from, and is to be correlated with, the earlier unmet need for love from the parent of the same sex, or rather, *the inability to receive such love, whether or not it was offered.*'[7]
6. 'This defensive detachment and its corresponding drive for renewed attachment imply that the homosexual condition is one of *same-sex ambivalence*...Firstly...the defensive detachment from the same-sex parental love-source will be marked by hostility, whether overt or latent, towards parental figures and...other members of the same sex. This hostility may be a component of actual sexual relationships....Likewise, in the male homosexual there is a search to fulfil hitherto unmet needs through the medium of a restored attachment,'[8] *which has become eroticised.*
7. 'The capacity for same-sex love is the natural healing process...The homosexual condition does not involve abnormal needs, but normal needs that have, abnormally, been left unmet in the ordinary process of growth.'[9]

A rigorous application of the criteria outlined earlier is not possible here, and, in particular, there seems to have been no work done on the application of biological theory or evidence to the Moberly theory. Much of the other findings, however, has either been explicitly addressed by Moberly, or appears to fit well within the theory. Her way of subsuming the classical Oedipal theory is worth quoting:

> The well-known 'mother fixation' of the male homosexual, which has been a standard ingredient of psychoanalytic theory from Freud onwards, strikes the present writer as being an effect rather than a cause. To be attached to one's mother is in itself entirely normal. However, if there is a defensive detachment from the father, the only remaining channel for attachment is that to

---

[7] Moberly, 6. Italics are mine, inserted to draw attention to the fact that unmet needs for love are not necessarily the fault of the parent concerned.
[8] Moberly, 6, 7, 9. The second set of italics is mine.
[9] Moberly, 18.

> the mother. What is normal when complemented by a father-attachment becomes abnormal when isolated from this.[10]

Biblically, the theory everywhere assumes the complementarity of the sexes built into human beings by the Creator, and the desirability of preserving or restoring a heterosexual orientation. It also preserves the connection, affirmed in Scripture, between disposition, on the one hand, and activity, on the other.

Some models of therapy aimed at re-orientation

Therapy aimed at re-orientation has come from a number of differing 'schools' within the practice of psychotherapy. Some, but not all, flow from a serious attempt to formulate a theory of homosexuality. Some must be seen, however, as *ad hoc* attempts to effect change.

1. Psychoanalytic or Freudian approaches try to return clients to their childhood Oedipal experiences, in order, belatedly, to resolve them. The expectation is that once this has been done, the orientation based upon those experiences will itself wither away.
2. The rational-emotive approach of Ellis has been employed in the attempt to re-orient lesbians by helping them overcome their fear of, and hostility towards males. There seems to be no reason why the same approach could not be employed with male homosexuals.
3. Classical conditioning has been used through associating homosexual responses with noxious experiences. According to John Court:

   > What was attractive is made undesirable by associating it with noxious (painful or unpleasant) experiences. This use of aversive techniques is scientifically attractive for its directness, its reliance on well-established scientific phenomena, and its observability. Nonetheless, the reported work of Max (1935), using painful electric shock, and later the use of the drug apomorphine by Freund (1960) has not been followed up. Dealing with the problem

---

[10] Moderly, 8.

symptomatically in this way did not take the patient's total adjustment into account and follow-up has proved disappointing.[11]

I would add that the danger here is that sexuality, in general, will be suppressed, rather than homosexuality in particular. Classical conditioning can prove a very blunt instrument where more complex personality issues are concerned.

4. Operant conditioning has done a little better than its 'cousin'. The training situation devised involves both the weakening of the homosexual response and the strengthening of a heterosexual response through anticipatory avoidance. Court elaborates as follows:

> The male patient knows that pictures will be projected on a screen and that following the appearance of an attractive male, a shock may be given unless an avoidance response is made. He may avoid by pressing a button which results in rejection of the slide and the appearance of a female instead. In this way males become associated with threat of pain and hence lose their attractive connotations, while females are associated with escape from pain and hence develop positive associations. The reverse associations can be used for female patients.
>
> The outcome of this type of treatment gives room for optimism that lasting change will become a real possibility. In 1967, MacCulloch and Feldman described the outcome of treating forty three patients (including two females). Thirty six completed treatment and when followed up a year later twenty five (58%) were significantly improved.[12]

My comment here is that though 'lasting change' may be a possibility, such change is likely to be change merely in *responses*, and that the deeper questions of relationship and motivation will not necessarily be dealt with. If the patient's 'total adjustment is taken into account' by some other form of therapy, then it could well be that operant conditioning could bring into line responses that were proving recalcitrant and deeply entrenched.

5. Systematic desensitization has been ulitised for purposes of re-orientation. Graded retraining has been employed to

---

[11] J.H. Court, 'Homosexuality: A Scientific and Christian Perspective', *Interchange*, Number 13, 32-3.

[12] Court, 33.

eliminate fear of the opposite sex, and relaxation to inhibit anxiety. To quote Court once again:

> Attention is devoted to the learned fear of the opposite sex. A graded retraining is provided in which mildly unattractive members of the opposite sex are associated (in fantasy or reality) with some kind of rewarding situation. (Progressively, more and more threatening fantasies are handled with equanimity as they are associated with pleasurable feelings.) Relaxation is commonly used to inhibit the anxiety which would otherwise be generated.[13]

Once again, if Moberly's theory is correct, fear of the opposite sex is nowhere near the heart of the homosexual condition. Where it occurs—and it is not a consistent feature—it is probably better to regard it, like the Oedipal factors, as a by-product, in which case my comment on operant conditioning would apply here: that it could feature as an ancillary 'mopping up' procedure.

6. Moberly's model of therapy follows on directly from her theoretical outline: 'Same-sex needs are to be fulfilled—according to the natural, God-given laws for human growth—before relating to the opposite sex as heterosexual'.[14] 'The defensive detachment vis-a-vis the same sex is to be undone, and unmet needs are to be met...Relationships and prayer may serve as the means towards this twofold goal.'[15]

The appropriate elements, then, in Moberly's therapy can be summarised as follows:

    a. Undoing the defensive detachment. Because negativity towards the same-sex parent has been transferred to members of the same sex in general, then these defensive attitudes may be worked through in any current same sex relationship. In addition, however, there will need to be work done on what David Seamands called 'the healing of memories'. The defensive detachment is an unresolved 'mourning process', and as such must be

---

[13] Court, 34.
[14] Moberly, 40.
[15] Moberly, 41, 42.

worked through. Forgiveness will play a central part in this, not in some self-generated way, but through the power of the Holy Spirit.

b. The importance and place of prayer. For Moberly prayer is at the heart of therapy, engaged in by all those involved, presumably by the client, by the counsellor, and jointly by both. A strong implication of this position is that prayer engages the personal relationship between the client and God as the loving Parent. Prayer will be the context, not only for forgiveness, mentioned above, but also for the overcoming of mistrust and the generation of trust.

c. The involvement of supportive same-sex heterosexual relationships is important in Moberly's scheme of therapy. Important examples are relationships with a substitute parent, with a heterosexual counsellor and with heterosexual peers. This 'innocent-sounding' listing of people carries a strong challenge for individual members of the Christian church; for every Christian, homosexually inclined, will need the close friendship both of parent-like heterosexuals, and same-sex heterosexual peers. But if such people are either generally uncaring, or, in particular homophobic, this basic resource for healing is removed. There will be no way in which the basic same-sex needs for attachment can be met without the eroticisation that constitutes the homosexual condition!

Religiously mediated change in homosexuals

What follows is a brief account of yet another form of therapy aimed at re-orientation. Because of its uniqueness and importance, however, there is a strong case for treating it separately. The article reporting this approach was written by E. Mansell Pattison and Myrna Loy Pattison, and was entitled:

' "Ex-Gays": Religiously Mediated Change in Homosexuals'.[16] There follows an extract from the synopsis, preceding the article.

> The authors evaluated 11 white men who claimed to have changed sexual orientation from exclusive homosexuality to exclusive heterosexuality through participation in a pentecostal church fellowship. Religious ideology and a religious community offered the subjects a 'folk therapy' experience that was paramount in producing their change. On the average their self-identification as homosexual occurred at age 11.[17] their change to heterosexual identification occurred at age 23, and their period of heterosexual identification at the time of this study was 4 years. The authors report 8 men became emotionally detached from homosexual identity in both behavior and intrapsychic process; 3 men were functionally heterosexual with some evidence of neurotic conflict...All subjects manifested major before-after changes...Substantial change in sexual orientation without explicit treatment and/or long term psychotherapy may be much more common than previously thought.[18]

The article is reported in a sober manner, and published within a prestigious refereed journal. It therefore must be taken seriously. The elements of this form of transformation would seem to be as follows:

1. We assume that the pentecostal church background would yield confident and expectant belief that God the Holy Spirit can bring about significant personal change in believers.
2. There is no doubt from the article that the scriptural attitude towards homosexuality is wholeheartedly accepted by the individuals concerned, and by the other church members.
3. It is also quite clear that participation in a warm accepting church fellowship was a significant factor in bringing about change. Attention has been drawn to the therapeutic effects of the corporate life of a church, especially by Lawrence Crabb, in his books and guide-

---

[16] *American Journal of Psychiatry* 137:12, December 1980, 1553-62.
[17] I cannot believe this figure; possibly it is a misprint. The text may be more reliable when it says 'All our subjects experienced defined homosexual proclivities before age 15'.
[18] Pattison and Pattison, 1553.

sheets, under the heading of 'Encouragement'.[19] Interestingly also, attention has been drawn to the counter-therapeutic effects of dysfunctional church families upon the individuals within them, in the work of Edwin Friedman, in *Generation to Generation: Family process in church and synagogue.*[20]

4. It is worth noting that these findings can well be brought under Moberly's category of 'relationships'—as well, of course, as that of prayer. Though Moberly's examples are all in terms of person-to-person relationships, the more solidary relationships, constituting what can well be called 'community', are a very natural extension of her basic approach to therapy. The beneficent effects noted would hopefully not be restricted to churches of a pentecostal persuasion, but would require a whole church ethos which was free of homophobic reactions, and which positively manifested an unmistakable loving warmth.

Hope

Nobody who is involved in research on homosexuality, nor anyone who is involved in clinical psychotherapy will claim that the re-orientation of homosexual clients is easy or frequent, but the fact is that such re-orientation occurs in some cases. And in this lies hope! From the standpoint of this paper, that hope lies in the power of God the Holy Spirit, expressed scientifically by an ever more adequate theory, therapeutically by ever more appropriate forms of procedure and personally by the loving interaction with clients of Christian therapists, mentors and friends, both individually and in church groups.

A brief survey has been presented here of Elizabeth Moberly's research-based and Christian theory of homosexuality. It seems to this writer that it is the most

---

[19] Especially publications culminating in *Effective Biblical Counseling*, Grand Rapids, Michigan: Zondervan, 1977.

[20] New York: The Guilford Press, 1985.

powerful and defensible available at this time; but, no doubt it will need to be modified, extended and corrected. In addition I have listed here a number of therapeutic procedures which have been employed which make some claim to a positive contribution. This is an era of intensive innovatory work in the field of psychotherapy, and some quite powerful procedures are emerging. With this movement come the twin challenges to Christian sifting and evaluation, on the one hand, and responsible use on the other. One frightening possibility inherent in more powerful procedures is personal domination and manipulation. The other, however, is more effective assistance for those who sincerely want re-orientation but find the struggle difficult. And in this lies genuine hope! I shall now mention a few procedures which may well have hopeful possibilities for re-orientation.

First, there is Primal Therapy. This approach was pioneered by Arthur Janov, whose major books on the subject appeared in the early 1970s.[21] For Janov, 'primal pains' refers to the hurt derived from early childhood where needs for affectionate holding and hugging have been absent and ignored, and where the child has been hushed, ridiculed or 'put down'. Central to the therapy are 'primals', in which key 'primal scenes' of early childhood are relived in a total, and often explosive manner, involving mind and body. Cure is thought to be effected by the systematic 'emptying' of the 'primal pool' of stored repressed emotions. Though Janov conceded that only some clients seemed to profit from the approach, nevertheless the impression is given that Primal Therapy was an adequate tool to deal with all 'neurosis', as he saw this, which included homosexuality.

Now Primal Therapy has been modified by its users and is frequently seen as one approach among others. While Moberly would agree that much derives from deprivation of affection in early childhood, it is very doubtful that she would classify homosexuality as 'neurosis', which has strong

---

[21] *The Primal Scream-Primal Therapy: The Cure for Neurosis;* New York: G.P. Putnam's Sons, 1970.
The Primal Revolution - Toward a Real World, New York: Simon and Schuster, 1972.

overtones of reality-avoidance. Nor, of course, would she emphasise, as a *central* procedure, the re-visiting of early childhood scenes; but then, as we have seen, neither would she rule it out. What she would do would be to contextualise them. One difficulty in the area is the emergence, in quite recent months, of the False Memory Syndrome, according to which clients suffering a good degree of emotional turmoil may have false memories triggered by counsellor-like figures, who suggest to them that they have suffered from various forms of abuse—at this stage sexual abuse. The discovery of the syndrome is not a denial that sexual abuse occurs; manifestly it does! But it does emphasise the need for caution in the way suggestions are made, and the caution would need to apply to Primal Therapy as to other procedures. Having said all of this, Primal Therapy remains a powerful tool for releasing repressed emotional material for those who, in the course of sexual re-orientation, are in need of this.

A second powerful procedure is one in which family dynamics are 'mapped' over several generations on both sides of a client's 'tree'. It is partly an 'understanding' factor that is important, in that it is enlightening to know the relational context from which, in part, one has emerged. But, especially where interviews are conducted, it may well be the 'reliving' engendered that can bring about quite powerful effects. No doubt factors of *identification* may be the key here, as they apply also in both parables and films. Whatever the dynamics, 'Family Therapy', understood in this way, holds considerable therapeutic possibilities for re-orientation.

Contemporary hypnotherapy is another approach with a potentially significant contribution. In its current form, hypnotherapy is neither demonic, nor occult, nor given to 'stagey' effects, nor used to dredge up otherwise inaccessible memories. (Such memories have now been proved to be extremely 'worked over' and unreliable!) Nor does the client necessarily have to become 'unconscious' and outside the possibility of conversational interaction with the therapist. Hypnosis merely relaxes the client so that intuitive, imaginative and affective factors are focussed and given the chance to make their creative contribution to an overall balanced adjustment of the person. In particular it can be used to loosen, or possibly even dissolve the rigidity of undesirable attitudes and orientations which would not otherwise be under conscious control. Its possibilities in tackling a homosexual orientation, therefore, are considerable.

Finally a word should be said about the very recent procedure called 'Eye Movement Desensitisation and Reprocessing'. From the observations of recent studies on sleep has come the conclusion that, when sleep is characterised by rapid eye-movements, a mental processing or sorting-out process is going on. This can be a mixture of current everyday happenings or of happenings from the past which are psychologically significant but have not been fully dealt with. Armed with the hypothesis that the eye movements are causally connected with the processing of events, psychologists guessed that if rapid eye movements were brought about in the *waking* state, a similar processing might occur. Though nothing has been firmly established yet, the indications look promising that here is a method whereby access can be gained to earlier experiences more quickly and more accurately than by hypnosis or other methods. If this is so, we have yet another powerful means by which the significant relationships and events leading to a homosexual orientation could be revisited and re-interpreted.

An important issue raised in the period of discussion following Philip Mitchell's paper, was whether realistic expectations for change in the responses of homosexual people would be restricted to changes in *behaviour*, and Philip himself was inclined to this view. From clinical experience of which I am aware, we may look for more inclusive changes than this at least in some people. And it is worth supporting this anecdotal report by repeating a sentence from the Pattison and Pattison study: 'The authors report (that) 8 men became emotionally detached from homosexual identity *in both behaviour and intrapsychic process*'.[22] Such a holistic outcome can be expected only, of course, when the therapy is concentrated on the development of the whole person rather

---

[22] Pattison and Pattison, 1553.

than exclusively on his or her sexual direction; and this, in turn, involves the whole web of personal relationships within which a person has identity, including relationship with God. Secondly, while accepting Moberly's finding that a homosexually oriented person will necessarily display some aspects of ambivalence, it will nevertheless be important that he or she should *want* re-orientation, even if, in some ways, personal change is unwelcome. There was a man mentioned in the Gospel of Mark, who said to Jesus 'I do believe, help me overcome my unbelief!' The parallel here might be: 'I do want to be changed; help me overcome my resistance to change!' In both cases we can hear Jesus saying, 'Everything is possible for the one who believes'.[23]

'In this life we have three great lasting qualities—faith, hope and love."[24] The three are strongly interconnected. The greatest of them is love, and one which is difficult in our modern world is hope. Those who live by faith and engage in acts of love may themselves display hope and infect others also with hope.

Exploring Further

1. You probably have a relative, a friend or a colleague who is homosexually inclined and is also a Christian. Could you explore, with him or her in fellowship, what tensions are felt, and whether some experiences in life are identified as having contributed to the present inclinations?
2. One factor in the paper which can assist in the process of reorientation is continuous and warm friendship from a heterosexual friend of the same sex. Would your present understanding of the homosexual disposition free you to offer and maintain such a friendship? Or, depending on respective ages, could you function as a substitute 'parent'?

---

[23] Mark 9:24b (New International Version).
[24] 1 Corinthians 13:13a (J.B. Phillips).

3. A further factor is participation in a warm accepting church fellowship. Especially if you are a pastor, are there ways of your congregation overcoming their homophobia, and becoming such a group?
4. What ministries within your church, or within your individual calling, could contribute to loving family relationships and especially to good times shared between mothers and their daughter and fathers and their sons?

COUNSELLING HOMOSEXUALS: THE THEORY AND PRACTICE OF THE ANGLICAN COUNSELLING CENTRE, SYDNEY

Michael Corbett-Jones
Director, Anglican Counselling Centre, Sydney

Synopsis

The counselling of homosexuals is one aspect of the counselling ministry offered by the Anglican Counselling Centre. Homosexual behaviour is understood as the outworking of an emotionally driven hope that unmet childhood needs for intimacy can be met in a present relationship. The hope is unrealistic but serves to maintain the repression of the painful childhood emotions.

Counselling is directed toward feeling the emotional pain, still present in the form of emotional memory. Counselling includes giving information about possible causes of the condition as well as the aim of the counselling process. Teaching is given on the Holy Spirit's role in enabling the person to choose to stop the inappropriate behaviour. Ceasing the behaviour is important for the health of the individual's relationship with God and facilitates access to the repressed painful emotion.

Various processes can be used to facilitate contact with the painful emotional memories. These are not described. Feeling the painful memories enables acceptance of the deprivation that evoked them and dissipates the emotion and the pain. Acceptance of the reality of the childhood hurt results in the giving up of the false hope that these needs can be met in a symbolic relationship in an adult context. This in turn results in a reduction of the need to seek out such relationships.

Progress in counselling requires faith, courage and persistence. The process will be longer or shorter depending on the degree of trauma experienced and the degree of resolution required.

Prologue

The counselling activity of the Anglican Counselling Centre provides for a wide range of human needs. The major thrust is toward marriage and family counselling - 8,000 hours provided in the last financial year. Personal counselling for a great variety of conditions, of which homosexuality is but one, added another 3,000 hours to the total for the same period.

As the range of human needs is wide, so is the range of counselling processes and procedures used by counsellors from time to time. While relationship counselling processes are different from personal counselling processes, there are common principles. Similarly, a theory and theology of the human condition and of how change occurs, undergirds the practice of counselling and the choice of the processes and procedures.

The subject of these papers is homosexuality. This particular paper focusses on the Anglican Counselling Centre's counselling response to an individual who seeks counselling help because of disturbing thoughts and/or behaviour of a homosexual kind.

Other papers have considered some possible causes of homosexual behaviour, including genetic influences and inadequacies in nurture. It is acknowledged that no-one can be certain about the cause(s) of homosexuality. The reality is that there is probably a multitude of factors leading to homosexual behaviour. If there is a genetic factor, it is not something the counsellor can focus on. Current behaviour and the effects of nurturing are the factors on which counselling can focus.

In meeting the client at his point of need, the counsellor comes with a view or hypothesis of how people come to behave the way they do. The counsellor will employ the counselling processes and procedures he/she believes will most readily help the client to a place of greater freedom, to think and behave in godly ways. If this outcome is not achieved, the counsellor must review the hypothesis and the processes and procedures. If this outcome is achieved (albeit in limited measure), the counsellor may be confirmed in the value of the hypothesis and the processes and procedures, while being open to influences that may modify these.

This paper aims to fulfil a request to present 'The Theory and Practice of the Anglican Counselling Centre' for the counselling of homosexuals.

Introduction

Dr Bill Andersen has mentioned in his paper the theory put forward by Moberly[1], that a homosexual disposition may arise from an eroticised need for the love not given by the parent of the same sex.

This accords with my own view that much homosexual behaviour is an unconscious, emotional needs-driven attempt to get unmet childhood intimacy needs satisfied in current adult contexts. It is an outworking of a need to fill a void: 'to get now what I didn't get then.' It is compensatory and is driven by the false hope that, 'I will get these needs met sometime, somewhere, with someone'. A failure in one current adult context results in a shift of the hope to another adult in another context. The sufferer will not allow himself to feel the pain of the unmet need. In fact, the hope that the need will be met, keeps him unaware of the pain.

Homosexual behaviour is only one expression or outworking of a needs driven false hope. There can be heterosexual expressions of the same false hope and there are many non-sexual ways of expressing it as well.

---

[1] E. R. Moberly, *Homosexuality: A New Christian Ethic*, (Cambridge: J. Clark, 1983), 5, 6.

The genesis of compensatory behaviour

In theorising about the causes of the homosexual condition, Moberly spoke generally about the condition possibly arising if the child's needs for love remain unmet through a disrupted attachment to the parent of the same sex.

The statement raises the questions, What are these needs for love? How may they be met and not met? and, What happens in the child whose needs for love are not met?

On touching

Ashley Montagu, cultural anthropologist and author of the well-known book 'Touching'[2], believes that tactile stimulation is vitally important for survival. The skin is the largest of the body organs and 'without the adequate stimulation of the skin that every human being must undergo in the womb and from the moment of birth, that human being will suffer massive privations such that their repair, if he or she happens to survive, will become increasingly more difficult the greater the length of time that is allowed to lapse'.[3] It is through being touched gently and lovingly that we learn emotionally that we are acceptable and accepted, that we are loved and lovable.

It was very meaningful to the leper and should be for us, that Jesus touched him *before* he 'cleansed' him rather than after (Mark 1:40-41). Jesus' touch said, 'I accept you just as your are'. Such acceptance is one expression of 'perfect' love. All humans need lots of it, especially children.

Don't all parents touch their children? A current client of mine, once a week bravely allows herself to feel a little more of the immense emotional and physical pain she carries in her body as a result of her parent's inability to show their love for her at any age, by caringly and lovingly touching her, holding her, cuddling and hugging her. Could she be imagining it?

---

[2] A. Montagu, *Touching*. (Harper & Row, 1978).
[3] Montegu, from the text of a lecture delivered in Los Angeles, October 19, 1975. *Journal of Primal Therapy*, Vol. III, No. 1, 1976.

Surely her mother touched her. She wrote to her mother to find out and received this in reply:

> I am not given to being demonstrative - not addicted to kissing and cuddling, which often seems to me not genuine and insincere. However, this does not mean I feel less affection.

I have no doubt that my client's mother did and does love her. The tragedy is, she was unable to express her love adequately and so my client's experience as a child was that of not feeling loved. This resulted in the child believing, on an emotional level, that she was not lovable—'there must be something wrong with me'.

My client is one of many who can attest to the immense amount of emotional pain experienced by a child who is not touched adequately. Perhaps her own mother suffered similarly as a child and was therefore unable to give her daughter what she herself had not received. It would have been too painful!

On intimacy

Touching is one of the vital ways love and acceptance are expressed. Intimate relating is another. Intimacy requires a safe relationship in which two people feel free to reveal themselves to each other in a personal way—thoughts, feelings, hopes and failures. Acceptance of the other's thoughts, feelings and perceptions, without judgment or criticism communicates acceptance of the person. Acceptance, of course, is not condoning, and the reverse is also true.

From earliest years, children need to know that they are accepted, with their particular thoughts, feelings and perceptions. Where this is not so, they will feel unacceptable and will hunger for intimacy and acceptance. The pain of this emotional hunger is as real as the pain of physical hunger and, not surprisingly, eating may become one way of attempting to satisfy it.

Worse than a parent leaving or dying, is the situation where a parent is around but never connecting with the child. The hope is kept alive but is never fulfilled. The pain is prolonged and chronic. Here is one man's expression of his pain and ambivalence in his love for his father:

> My father married his work and it had the excitement of a mistress. I don't think my mother or our family were ever second place in my father's life. I believe for him we didn't exist at all. I grew up spending inordinate amounts of time thinking about my father, yet never really knowing him. I hate him for this and I miss him deeply.[4]

Several male homosexuals, in the context of a counselling relationship, have acknowledged that sex was not the attraction, but the hope of intimacy with a male.

On coping with emotional pain

It is hard for adults whose protective mechanisms have been developed over years to realise how deeply children experience emotions of all kinds, and to appreciate how painful it is to a child to feel emotions such as fear, worthlessness, abandonment, loneliness, sadness and so on. The emotional centres of the brain are viable from the earliest months of development, long before speech and reason.[5]

Some emotional pain is too painful to feel. It must be coped with in some other way. One coping mechanism for dealing with the pain of deprivation is to deny the need for what is not provided, 'I don't need to be hugged, that's sissy stuff'. This way of coping may be reinforced by emphasising the opposite, 'I'm tough'.

Another way of coping is to avoid the pain of the unmet need by developing a hope that the need will be met, 'if only I keep trying and looking'. Both boys and girls who do not feel loved by their father will be very vulnerable to the offers of

---

[4] A. W. Schaef and D. Farrell, *The Addictive Organization*, (San Francisco: Harper & Row 1988).

[5] K. H. Pribram, *Languages of the Brain* (Monterey, Ca.: Brooks/Coles, 1971).

intimacy from another male. It is tragically common to see a love-starved child attempting to build a relationship with a teacher or other friendly adult. All too often this vulnerability is exploited.

The unreal hope

The theory that undergirds the Anglican Counselling Centre's approach to homosexuals is based on the hypothesis that the coping mechanism that leads to homosexual thoughts and behaviour is that which seeks to avoid pain by developing an unreal hope. (This unreal hope can lead to other kinds of inappropriate behaviour as well, not necessarily homosexual.)

A male adolescent whose father could not be appropriately affectionate and emotionally intimate may transfer his hope of having these needs met to a symbolic father figure—a school teacher or a sporting hero. Most adolescent males experience some ambiguity in their attachments during adolescence. These attachments are likely to be stronger in a homosexual direction where father intimacy has been scarce in childhood.

Should an adolescent with such a strong attachment also have physical contact with this male, such contact will inevitably stir up the longings for the physical intimacy that was not given in childhood. On an emotional level, a hope is activated; 'at long last these needs will now be met at this time, in this relationship'. It is a false hope because the needs that were unmet by our primary caregivers cannot subsequently be met in another relationship.

While early needs cannot be satisfied subsequently, the hope and longing that they can be seems compelling. The intense power of the emotional longing, the hope of the hunger being met, the ache that the void be filled, has led many normally circumspect men and women (including Christian men and women) to abandon their beliefs and sometimes their families, to pursue the hope that their deep childhood longings and yearnings for emotional intimacy can be satisfied. This may be in a heterosexual or a homosexual relationship, depending on whether the deprivation was in relation to the parent of the same or opposite sex.

The painful dissonance

When human beings behave in ways that are contrary to their beliefs and values, the resultant conflict causes its own pain. Our need to be consistent and congruent with ourselves makes it hard to live with such internal divisions. To reduce the anxiety caused by this tension we will either stop the behaviour we disapprove of and maintain our beliefs and values, or we will continue our behaviour and adjust our beliefs and values. Adjustment of beliefs and values is accomplished by the process of rationalising—'it's not really wrong', 'everybody does it', 'nothing's black and white', 'this is real love', 'nobody's perfect, they're all hypocrites anyway'.

Compassion for those caught in this dilemma

If a person has longings and urges he disapproves of and does everything he knows how to rid himself of them without success, what can he do? If he can't live with the tension of the dissonance and he can't quell the longings and urges, he has only one recourse. He has to change his beliefs. His need to accept himself with his urges and behaviour may strongly influence his way of understanding the biblical teaching on homosexuality and the origins of his urges.

If the sufferer believes the urges are due entirely to some genetic arrangement, the sufferer may reason that, as he has no responsibility in the acquisition of the malady, fairness requires that he be allowed a fulfilling sexual life like anybody else. This may then become the platform from which the scriptural teaching on the subject is read and interpreted.

This of course is a rationalisation. Although it is understandable, the point made in previous papers holds. How we have become what we are is irrelevant. We are still responsible for the way we express what we are, for our behaviour. It behoves all of us to draw on the grace of God to conform our behaviour to the will of God. Yet, this is a painful position for a Christian homosexual who is tempted constantly to get his unmet childhood needs for intimacy satisfied in a forbidden homosexual relationship. He feels the pain and guilt of disobedience on top of his other pain.

It may be argued that this is true for every Christian. I argue that while all Christians are subject to temptation, temptations to get intimacy needs met in ungodly ways come stronger and harder for those whose basic needs for love, affection and intimacy were not adequately satisfied in childhood. The deprivations give Satan a handle to use to tempt the sufferer. It is harder for some to live the Christian life than it is for others. It is important to understand that only God knows what difficulties any of us is facing and for what reasons. Assessing culpability for behaviour is God's prerogative and God fortunately 'remembers that we are dust and does not treat us as we deserve' (Ps 103:10, 14).

A way forward

What help is there for a homosexual (or any other person struggling with a need to compensate in some way for the deprivations of their early years) who is stuck in this dilemma? Some say, 'Look to God. He can meet every need. He is sufficient for you. In him you will find fulfilment and have all your needs met.' This sounds right but needs to be examined.

When God made Adam he made him with a need that was not satisfied simply in his relationship with God. 'It is not good for the man to be alone. I will make a helper suitable for him.' (Gen 2:18) God met Adam's need by making 'a helper suitable for him'.

Similarly, God has provided for the needs of babies and children by giving them caring mothers and fathers to nurture them and to love them. The reality of living in a fallen world is that those whom God has provided don't always do the job.

What response can we expect from God in this situation? He will not meet this need (for the time has long passed for that) but he will help us face the pain we carry with us as a result of that need not being met. When we have faced the pain, which is a present reality in our body and memory, we won't have to employ mechanisms to avoid it.

Facing the pain of unmet needs

This is not the place to describe in any detail any particular method or process for helping people to release old, stored, emotional pain. Dr Andersen has outlined some of these in his paper and there are others.

It is important to note that 'facing the pain' involves feeling the painful emotion. Rationally identifying that emotion (if you could) is not the same as feeling it. Rational processes are as different to emotional processes as seeing is to hearing. There is only one way to dissipate a painful emotional memory and that is to FEEL it.[6]

Some therapists can allow clients to feel old pain in order to let it go because they have felt and let go much of their own. Other therapists cannot encourage clients to feel old pain, perhaps because they haven't come to terms with their own.

Similarly, reading about this process strikes a chord for some, while others recoil from it. These personal reactions inevitably colour our attitude to the therapy process, to its theory and practice.

Feeling the emotional pain caused by the trauma is an integral part of the process and leads to a more complete contact with that trauma. This results in an acceptance of the reality of the situation, as it was perceived by the child at that time. When this childhood view of the situation emerges from its hidden place, into the now adult consciousness, it can be assessed for what it is. This assessment can result in an integrated acceptance that the need was not met then and therefore never will be. 'I will never get this need met' can be the beginning of a grieving process that will result in the abandonment of the false hope that someone, somewhere, some day, will fill the void.

---

[6] M. Corbett-Jones, 'Memories Recalled in Therapy'. Unpublished Research Project (Macquarie University, 1988).

The abandonment of the false hope results in an abatement of the pressure to compensate.

Counselling the homosexual

In Andrew Shead's paper in this volume, mention has been made of Dr John Court's identification of a minority of homosexuals who believe it inappropriate to engage in homosexual behaviour and who wish to change their orientation, if that were possible. Clearly, this is the group for whom counselling is appropriate.

A place for explanation

By the time sufferers are prepared to seek counselling help, they have often reached a level of despair, hopelessness and confusion that must be lifted before counselling can proceed. I have found that an explanation of the theory presented in this paper can bring profound relief and raise hope. The explanation of the 'false hope' rings a bell and many clients immediately confirm the experience of inadequate attachment to the parent of the same sex. Having a plausible explanation for the condition raises the possibility that the condition can be relieved.

Ceasing the inappropriate behaviour

The client who is struggling with behaviour that is inappropriate—homosexual behaviour, overeating, cross dressing, drinking, pornographic viewing, visiting prostitutes—is helped to stop this during the therapy process for two reasons.

The first is, it's ungodly and damages the client's relationship with God.

The second is, it ameliorates the underlying emotional pain, and therefore makes access to it more difficult. As progress is achieved through contacting and feeling that pain, the more available it is, the more progress can be made.

When we ask clients to stop the behaviour, they will say they have tried to do so, many times, without success. We will join with them in acknowledging that their experience has been, 'the good I want to do, I do not do. The evil I do not want, is what I do' (Rom 7:19).

The grace and gift of God through Jesus Christ

Time is taken to teach the client that the benefit of Christ's death is not only forgiveness of sin and reconciliation to God, it is also the ability to 'live by the Spirit and not gratify the desires of the sinful nature' (Gal 5:16).

It is important that the client knows that the Holy Spirit's supernatural work is to 'subdue the flesh' or 'put to death the misdeeds of the body' (Rom 8:13). This is because Jesus has 'disarmed the powers and authorities' and 'made a public spectacle of them, triumphing over them by the cross' (Col 2:15). Our human nature, through which Satan tempts us by making sin attractive, has been robbed of its power (Rom 6:6), just as Satan has been robbed of his power. Time is taken to ensure that the client understands that we do not resist temptation by using our wills to try harder not to give in; rather we use our wills to invite the Holy Spirit to do the supernatural work that only he can do. We ask the Holy Spirit to subdue our sinful nature to make the sin unattractive, so that we do not want to do it.

At the moment of temptation the client is encouraged to pray a prayer like this:

> Lord, this behaviour I am imagining is so attractive. Left to myself, by myself, I will give in. I am asking you to do your work in me. By your Holy Spirit, make this behaviour unattractive, so that I do not want to do it.

This is an honest, biblical prayer. It acknowledges the reality of the sinfulness of our flesh and depends entirely on Christ's triumph over Satan to deal with the tempter and the temptation.

Clients who pray in this way are shocked when their prayer is answered. Discovering that the pleasure used to ameliorate the pain has gone, they now feel the pain. At this point the client needs great faith to believe that if he gives up his long established way of gaining pleasure and avoiding the pain, God will give him something better in its place.

Coaching and encouragement

As would be expected, clients take two steps forward and one step back. Sometimes the counselling session is spent reviewing and reaffirming the reality of the Spirit's power and working through resistances to asking the Holy Spirit to be powerful in making the sin unattractive. Sometimes it is spent accessing the pain that emerges when the 'acting out' behaviour has been abandoned. Sometimes it is spent struggling to exercise the faith needed to believe God can and will provide something better. In reality, when the pain is felt and let go, God's love is there. It has been there all the time. The emotional pain and the beliefs that attend it, have been like a cloud blocking out the sun. When the cloud goes the sunshine is experienced, yet it was there all along. 'Putting off the old', in order to 'put on the new', may include more than we had previously thought.

Feeling the pain

The dissipation of pain left over from childhood can be a short or a long process, depending on how much pain is there to be felt. In cases of prolonged deprivation or sexual abuse, it can take years.

The experience of one homosexual client is worth mentioning here, as it is true of many. Having arrived at the point of giving up on inappropriate sexual behaviour, having wrestled with the fear of being left with nothing pleasurable, having reaffirmed faith in God to provide something different and better, this client allowed himself to feel some of his hidden emotional pain. He felt this in the context of his relationship with his father as he experienced it as a young boy. In his mind's eye, he could see his father as he was then and began to feel the longings that he had for his father at that time. As he allowed himself to feel the ache for his father's touch and affirmation, he recognised that this was the feeling he often experienced in adult life and avoided by searching out a homosexual relationship in which (he hoped) the need would be met and the pain ameliorated.

On facing the truth

We are encouraged throughout Scripture to celebrate truth, to face it, accept it, live in it and live by it.

Through this process we are encouraging people to face the truth of their emotional experiences, to allow painful childhood memories to emerge into full adult awareness, so that they can at long last be processed and put aside. Only then will they cease to powerfully distort perceptions, fuel desires and influence behaviour from a hidden place.

In the measure God gives us grace to do this, we find the freedom to behave appropriately as a spontaneous expression of our redeemed personality. This is different from behaving appropriately as an act of will, contrary to our compulsive urges. We are truly free when we behave appropriately, through the Spirit's power, out of an integrated personality. None of us is there yet. It is for each of us to take our next step forward, as God prompts us and enables us.

Exploring further

1. What is the difference between 'wholeness' and 'holiness'? Where, in the counselling approach outlined above, are these two qualities addressed?
2. 'The love and affection of the people in the church, especially the minister and his wife, will offset the effects of childhood neglect.' Evaluate this statement in the light of the operation of the 'false hope' and the power of Christian love and compassion.

3. It is better to simply ask God for healing, rather than dredge up old pain and hurts. Discuss.
4. In what ways is the counselling approach outlined above different from any other with which you may be familiar? In what ways is it the same?

COUNSELLING THE CHURCH

David Peterson
Head of the Department of Ministry, Moore College

Synopsis

Counselling the church about homosexuality will mean more than convincing one another about Scripture's condemnation of homosexual activity. We need to become aware of the pain experienced by those who would serve Christ but feel themselves powerfully attracted to those of the same sex. We need to be reminded of the great difference that belief in the gospel can make to a person's identity and sexual behaviour. But we also need to consider how the transforming work of the Holy Spirit might continue in the local congregation as a 'healing community' for all.

Many of us will be encouraged to know that there are experienced counsellors to whom we can recommend a variety of people seeking help. But 'passing the buck' to others is all too easy. In one way or another, we must all address the particular issue of pastoral care for homosexuals *within our churches*. My concern is especially for those who acknowledge that homosexual behaviour is condemned by Scripture, who seek to be chaste, but feel constrained to be totally secretive about their struggle. They may share their dilemma with one or two fellow Christians whom they feel they can trust. Beyond that, they would not dare to identify themselves to other Christians because of the reaction they might receive. Heterosexual Christians need to accept responsibility for the barriers they create in this regard. They need to be stirred to love and care for all who would serve the Lord Jesus, making no invidious distinctions, but working out the practical implications of the gospel for the spiritual growth and development of all.

The suffering of homosexuals

Someone who knows the scene well has put it like this. 'Many gays are figures of pathos. Often filled with self loathing, deep frustration and guilt. Unable (as they see it) to love those they are meant to love, they are drawn towards those whom it is forbidden to love. This is to say nothing of the hurt and embarrassment of friends/family if they choose to love, or accidentally slip up. I was speaking to a boy recently who told his grandmother he was gay. She replied that he was on his way to hell. Many indeed die in a hellish way, wasting away in significant discomfort with AIDS. Many gays are unable to sustain long-term relationships and, as their physical beauty fades, so they retreat into a shadowy existence, like Steppenwolf in the Herman Hesse novel of that name. What do you say to an 18 year old who confesses a strong homosexual attraction, given the very poor statistics on reorientation? No matter which way you look at it, he is in for a good deal of pain if he hangs in as a Christian. Sadly, many seek the solace and comfort of older (gay) men, who show them love and compassion and affection, establishing and reinforcing improper sexual behaviour patterns.'

Where ministers and churches are clear about the Bible's condemnation of homosexual practices it is obviously more difficult for those with a homosexual orientation to find the support and encouragement they need. Their isolation and loneliness inevitably exacerbates sexual tension and heightens the likelihood of 'at risk' behaviour. They look for a place of love and acceptance in the church but feel marginalised and alienated because they only ever hear negative statements about homosexuality.[1] A friend of mine put it like this: 'Many genuinely value relationships with young people, being drawn to them for emotional rather than sexual reasons. Many have had profitable ministries with youth. Yet their prognosis is poor. The sheer emotional

---

[1] L. Pierson, *No-Gay Areas? Pastoral Care of Homosexual Christians* (Bramcote, Nottingham: Grove, second edition, 1992), 5, observes: 'When the world outside is harsh and cold, small wonder that gay clubs thrive, offering understanding, acceptance, care, love..., in London alone there are more than 100'.

energy involved in covering up, watching their tracks, constantly hiding what they really feel themselves to be, paranoid fear of exposure and lack of supportive relationships eventually take their toll'. Depression, burnout, compromise, apostasy, and even suicide have resulted for those who find the lonely struggle too great. In this category, of course, we must include clergy who have lived with the temptation to engage in a homosexual lifestyle as a dominant pressure in their ministries.

Attraction, identity and sexual expression

The whole thrust of the gay scene is to help people accept what they are and choose positive gay role models as a way of forming their identity. So they subtly make the connection between attraction, identity and sexual expression. The mood of our society is such that people are readily convinced by this logic. If you feel yourself attracted to a member of the same sex, you are a homosexual and the only way to find fulfilment is to throw off the restrictions others might impose on you and indulge in a homosexual lifestyle. What alternative do we have to offer as the community of Christ's people? If someone is attracted to a member of the same sex, do we simply conclude that such a person is 'a homosexual' and write them off as beyond hope? How does God view a Christian who has homosexual desires? What does being in Christ mean for our sexual identity? Does sexual attraction really form identity and inevitably lead to certain behaviour?

Implicitly, we often make the mistake of putting homosexuals into a separate category. We consider that their identity will be so strongly formed by their sexual orientation that they cannot be Christians in the same sense as heterosexuals. But this is not logical. The NT teaches us that our essential identity as Christians is formed by Christ and the gospel. 'If anyone is in Christ, there is a new creation: everything old has passed away; see, everything has become new!' (2 Cor 5:17). Paul goes on to argue that this is so because God reconciled us to himself through Christ and has given to his ambassadors the ministry of reconciliation. As the message of reconciliation is proclaimed and received, God's great work of renewal begins in those who believe. In Jesus we become 'the righteousness of God' (2 Cor 5:21).

The potential for change

Paul reminds the Corinthian Christians that some of them had been 'fornicators, idolaters, adulterers, male prostitutes, sodomites, thieves, the greedy, drunkards, revilers, robbers' (1 Cor 6:10).[2] It is extremely important to note that he puts heterosexual and homosexual sin together with other expressions of rebellion against God. Warning the Corinthians not to act like pagans, the apostle insists that those who persist in the lifestyles that he mentions will not inherit the kingdom of God. But there had been a remarkable change of behaviour on the part of his readers. 'This is what some of you *used to be*', he says. 'But you were washed, you were sanctified, you were justified in the name of the Lord Jesus Christ and in the Spirit of our God.' (1 Cor 6:11)

Here the notion of being 'sanctified' or 'consecrated' to God is viewed as another dimension of becoming a Christian. Being cleansed from the defilement of sin and justified through faith in Jesus is closely linked with being set apart for a new relationship with God through the inner working of the Holy Spirit. The Corinthians were separated from their former lifestyle by being forgiven, cleansed and accepted by God. The Spirit worked through the preaching of the gospel to give them a new identity, a new hope and a new desire to please God. So the call of the apostle is for believers to live out their new status in holiness. Instead of uniting themselves with prostitutes of any sort, Paul goes on to say that they should treat their bodies as 'a temple of the Holy Spirit'. As those

---

[2] G. W. Fee, *The First Epistle to the Corinthians*, NICNT (Grand Rapids: Eerdmans, 1987), 243-4, provides a helpful discussion of the two terms relating to homosexual behaviour in 1 Cor 6:10 and concludes that the first most likely denotes consenting homosexual youths ('male prostitutes') and the second more generally homosexual offenders ('sodomites').

who have been 'bought with a price', they are to seek ways of actively glorifying God with their bodies.

> In the NT the place for gay sex, if anywhere, is in the past. The Gay Movement are simply wrong when they imply that it is impossible for those with homosexual leanings to resist the homosexual act. The gospel includes the power to change our lifestyle, even if a gay orientation sometimes remains.[3]

This teaching needs to be understood by every member of our churches. As the Spirit enables believers to work out what it means to be 'in Christ', attitudes and behaviour will be transformed in different areas of their lives (cf. Col 3:1-17). But only when we see the Lord Jesus face to face will we be completely like him. The view that we can somehow be morally perfect in this life is a dangerous misreading of the NT. Nevertheless, everyone who has the hope of ultimate transformation in Christ 'purifies himself, just as he is pure' (1 Jn 3:3). And the risen and ascended Christ provides the resources to live a pure or sanctified life, as we await the fulfilment of his purposes for us in the new creation. We *all* have to live with the tension of being hopeful about the change God can effect in us in the present but not expecting the change to be completely as we might desire. Christians are called to live in hope, acknowledging with gratitude what God has already done for them in Christ and trusting that his Holy Spirit is powerfully at work in their lives.

Of course, individual Christians will have different areas of pressure, temptation and difficulty, according to their natures and personal experience. When they turn to Christ, many bring scars and terrible hurts from their childhood or from broken relationships. These are not always acknowledged or dealt with in a satisfactory way, even by mature Christians. It is at this point that the need for special counselling may emerge.

We must beware of minimising the effect that the Holy Spirit can have on us, working through the ministry of God's word and the Christian fellowship to transform us. It would be wrong to suggest that we all need some form of professional

---

[3] Pierson, 14.

counselling before we can mature as Christians. But some people are so emotionally damaged that they cannot accept the full implications of the gospel for themselves or believe that God can change them. Some are so afraid of identifying their hurts and desires that they cannot open themselves to the informal and untrained help that may be offered in the local church. Various defence mechanisms can certainly prevent us from understanding our own attitudes and behaviour patterns. Consequently, it can be helpful to find someone who is skilled at facilitating contact with painful emotional memories. An experienced counsellor may be the channel by which the Holy Spirit enables some Christians to understand their motivation and modify certain behaviour patterns.

The promise of Scripture is that all believers can be 'transformed into the same image, from one degree of glory to another; for this comes from the Lord, the Spirit' (2 Cor. 3:18). So we should see one another in the same light, as those in need of God's forgiveness, healing and transformation. All need to discern how our sexuality and our relationships with others have been marred because we were born into a race fallen from a true relationship with God. Sin is insidious in its effect, even in the lives of those who have been converted!

This is very humbling and particularly difficult for those Christians who have unbiblical ways of classifying people (e.g., in terms of their backgrounds or in terms of the kind of temptation they experience). Is someone tempted to homosexual behaviour really a worse sinner than someone tempted to heterosexual adultery? We should be optimistic about what God can accomplish in the lives of each and every one of our fellow believers. On the other hand, we should be realistic about their need for every encouragement and support in running the race and fighting the spiritual battle. But how can Christians with a homosexual orientation find that help if they remain isolated and unrecognised in our midst?

The church as a healing community

This is not a prominent perspective in Evangelical circles, perhaps because many of us have unduly individualistic views of the Christian life. We rightly stress the need for personal conversion and encourage personal discipleship to Christ in everyday life. The local congregation is important because it can help me grow in my knowledge of God and can stir me up to love and good works! But this expectation is often limited to what the sermon or the church service can achieve. Few seem to anticipate that God might comfort, challenge or change them through the relationships formed with others in the Christian family. Furthermore, few see their membership of a church as an opportunity to contribute to the spiritual life and development of others. There is little concern to build up the congregation as the body of Christ.

To speak of the church as a healing community is another way of propounding the NT doctrine of edification, with a particular focus on what the Bible and the Holy Spirit can do in our ministry to one another. When the Spirit inspires people to teach and care for others in a congregational context, God moves them towards the ultimate goal which he has for them, which is to 'come to the unity of the faith and of the knowledge of the Son of God, to maturity, to the measure of the full stature of Christ.' (Eph 4:13) Before we start talking to our churches about the pastoral care of any particular group, we need to help them recover this biblical perspective on their life and witness as a totality.

Dr. Elizabeth Moberly believes that *counselling the church* is one of the most important, yet most neglected items on the pastoral agenda. She is especially concerned that congregations be delivered from the frigid embarrassment, anger and ostracism that is so often shown to homosexuals. She longs for churches to become communities of acceptance and healing, of forgiven and forgiving people:

> The church as a whole needs help in reassessing its attitudes. Counselling on this scale becomes in effect a task of re-education, so that the church may be recalled to its vocation as a healing community. It is important for Christians (and society in general) to face up to their responsibility for the irrational manifestations of

homophobia. To state that homosexual activity is inappropriate is one thing; to act with fear and hostility towards known homosexuals is quite another matter. The latter is not justified by the former - either logically, or on the principles of the Christian gospel, which commends love and forgiveness, not hostility. The homosexual issue is a testing-ground not merely for ethical discussion, but for the very ability to live out the gospel.[4]

Conversion to Christ will not necessarily 'cure' people of homosexuality, but God-honouring relationships within the Christian fellowship may facilitate remarkable change and growth. Dr. Moberly insists that same-sex love is a legitimate developmental drive that has not been appropriately met in the childhood experience of some people. 'Even if homosexual activity is inappropriate, that does not imply that the capacity for same-sex love is abnormal or pathological or deviant. It is entirely normal and legitimate on a developmental perspective. Same-sex love is the *solution* to unmet developmental needs. It is not the problem'.[5] The practical implication of this theory is that increased contact with members of the opposite sex will not resolve and fulfil same-sex developmental deficits. These can only be met in helpful relationships with members of the same sex. The process of counselling should focus on *same-sex relational needs* and on resolving underlying ambivalence towards members of the same sex. 'To block the capacity for same-sex love, as distinct from checking its sexual expression, is to block the very process of healing the homosexual condition.'

Dr. Moberly argues that a church with an adequate theology of friendship would have no difficulty in understanding and forwarding this process:

> It is a sad comment on much contemporary church life that the depth of relationships leaves much to be desired. This general difficulty becomes particularly acute for the known homosexual, who may well be forced into a marginalised position in church life,

---

[4] E. R. Moberly, 'First Aid in Pastoral Care XV. Counselling the Homosexual', *Expository Times* 96 (1985), 261-6 (264), reprinted in a pamphlet, *Counselling the Homosexual*, by the True Freedom Trust, PO Box 592, London SE4 1EF.

[5] Ibid, 262. She has argued her case more fully in *Psychogenesis* (Routledge & Kegan Paul, 1983) and *Homosexuality: A New Christian Ethic* (James Clarke, 1983).

if not altogether excluded from fellowship. How many heterosexual men, for instance, would be prepared to offer a deep and sustaining friendship to a homosexual man? Unfortunately, many heterosexuals would fear for their reputation. Not only may the opportunity for a mutually valuable relationship be missed, but the hesitant heterosexual bears a considerable responsibility for leaving the homosexual with no alternative but to seek relationships with other homosexuals.[6]

Heterosexuals may also fear homosexuals because of their own sexual ambiguity or latent homosexuality. When this is not acknowledged, projection may take place as a psychological defence mechanism, so that what is unacceptable is strongly condemned in others, rather than in oneself.

What can we do?

We must first ask ourselves how we would react to a friend, colleague or member of our family who revealed to us that he or she was a homosexual. In other words, it is important for us to recognise and acknowledge any homophobia that we may have. Until we sense that it is a privilege and a great expression of trust for someone to confess their sexual struggles to us, we are in no position to help them. If we are guilty of homophobia in any form we need to discover and deal with it. Lance Pierson has exposed the dimensions of the problem in this way:

> Homophobia is far more widespread than homosexuality. It is not recognised as a pathological condition; so it is largely untreated and unconfessed. Yet those with gay feelings instantly detect it. It wounds them, hammering into them that they are unlovable, unforgivable, unwelcome. We drive them away from our churches, especially evangelical churches, where they assume they will be condemned. We distort their view of God by implying that he shares our hate of gays. Our passing remarks and sweeping

---

[6] Ibid, 265. Many of the practical implications of being a healing community for homosexuals are explored by Pierson, 15-24. Pierson endorses the approach of Moberly.

generalisations in favour of 'a hard line against gays' force many silent sufferers into the misery of secret loneliness.[7]

Only when we have examined ourselves and repented of wrong attitudes and behaviour can we encourage homosexuals in our sphere of influence to make themselves known to us and offer them the friendship and support they need.

Second, I believe that we should be regularly instructing and encouraging our churches about what the Word and the Spirit can do in the fellowship of God's people. This must include an emphasis on the power of forgiveness, acceptance and love to transform individuals and relationships within the body of Christ. Members of the congregation need to be encouraged to open their homes and their hearts to one another, to provide a genuinely caring fellowship for all. Within this framework, any negative teaching about homosexual practices and the gay lifestyle must be complemented by positive teaching about Christian life and values. Homosexuals sometimes experience a change of sexual orientation through counselling and therapy. For others, however, healing comes in finding acceptance and peace about their sexual orientation and learning how to live fulfilled lives as servants of Christ and members of his family. We need to foster positive attitudes to singleness in our churches by encouraging relationships based on Christ's love, as a way of enabling the problem of 'aloneness' to be healed.

Third, I believe Evangelicals ought to be initiating and supporting organisations like the True Freedom Trust in England. This was founded at Merseyside in 1977 by Martin Hallett and Canon L. Roy Barker. Martin was involved in a homosexual lifestyle for over nine years before the Lord Jesus dramatically changed his life. In 1984 TFT helped to set up a similar ministry in London known as Turnabout. In 1991 TFT and Turnabout merged. TFT now has a staff of several full and part-time workers and volunteers. It is governed by 8

---

[7] *No-Gay Areas?*, 7. 'We have the gall to call homosexual sufferers to healing', he notes. 'Yet there is no health in *us*! Make clean our hearts, and renew a right spirit within us.'

trustees and a council of reference. The organisation is maintained financially by the support of members, who are committed to the ideals of TFT and receive a regular newsletter.

TFT exists to provide counselling (in person and by phone) for those struggling with homosexuality and other sexual problems. They also offer help to relatives, spouses and friends. A variety of books, articles, testimonies, cassettes and videos are available for purchase or loan. TFT representatives are also available to speak about the work and to share what they believe God teaches about sexuality. They are significantly involved in educating and encouraging churches in this matter. Support groups, called Turnabout Groups, exist across the UK so that Christians can meet in confidence to share, learn and pray together, whatever their sexuality. Members of these groups are expected to agree with the aims and beliefs of TFT. The aim of each group is to complement and encourage deep Christian sharing in the home church of every member, not to replace it.

TFT is linked with similar agencies in other countries through an association called Exodus International. Exodus ministries in the South Pacific region are co-ordinated from Brisbane by an organisation called Liberty.

As those who speak strongly against homosexual practices from a biblical point of view, Evangelicals should be in the forefront of those trying to provide help and a holistic biblical perspective on sexuality. As those who believe that God can change people and give them resources to lead a godly life in a whole range of circumstances, we should be encouraging our churches to have a wider vision of themselves and of what God might be pleased to do in them and through them.

Exploring further

1. What do you think are the main reasons for 'homophobia'?
2. How can we help members of our churches to be better pastoral carers, especially with those who may be homosexually oriented?
3. How can we better provide for the needs of single adults in our churches?
4. What can we do to teach and support adolescents in our churches who may be experiencing ambiguity about their sexual orientation?